A–D
Afghans to Dominicans

Titles in the series

A–D
Afghans to Dominicans

E–H
Ecuadoreans to Haitians

I–L
Indians to Laotians

M–P
Mexicans to Puerto Ricans

R–V
Russians to Vietnamese

The NEWEST Americans

A–D
Afghans to Dominicans

GREENWOOD PRESS
Westport, Connecticut · London

Library of Congress Cataloging-in-Publication Data

Creative Media Applications
  The newest Americans
    p. cm.–(Middle school reference)
  Includes bibliographical references and index.
  ISBN 0-313-32553-7 (set: alk. paper)–0-313-32554-5 (v.1)–0-313-32555-3 (v.2)–
  0-313-32556-1 (v.3)–0-313-32557-X (v.4)–0-313-32563-4 (v.5)
  1. Immigrants–United States–Juvenile literature–Encyclopedias.
  2. United States–Emigration and immigration–Juvenile literature–Encyclopedias.
  3. Minorities–United States–Juvenile literature–Encyclopedias.
  [1. Immigrants–United States–Encyclopedias. 2. United States–Emigration and
  immigration–Encyclopedias. 3. Minorities–Encyclopedias.] I. Series.
  JV6455.N48 2003
  304.8'73'03–dc21   2002035214

British Library Cataloguing in Publication Data is available.

Library of Congress Catalog Card Number: 2002035214
ISBN: 0–313–32553–7 (set)
       0–313–32554–5 (vol. 1)
       0–313–32555–3 (vol. 2)
       0–313–32556–1 (vol. 3)
       0–313–32557–X (vol. 4)
       0–313–32563–4 (vol. 5)

First published in 2003

Greenwood Press, 88 Post Road West, Westport, CT 06881
An imprint of Greenwood Publishing Group, Inc.
www.greenwood.com

Printed in the United States of America

∞™

The paper used in this book complies with the Permanent Paper Standard issued by the National Information Standards Organization (Z39.48–1984).

10 9 8 7 6 5 4 3 2 1

A Creative Media Applications, Inc. Production
WRITER: Sandy Pobst
DESIGN AND PRODUCTION: Fabia Wargin Design, Inc.
EDITOR: Susan Madoff
COPYEDITOR: Laurie Lieb
PROOFREADER: Betty Pessagno
INDEXER: Nara Wood
ASSOCIATED PRESS PHOTO RESEARCHER: Yvette Reyes
CONSULTANT: Robert Asher, University of Connecticut

Sincere thanks to Dr. Farid Younos of the Afghan Coalition in Fremont, California, for his contributions to the Afghan chapter. (Afghan Coalition, 39155 Liberty Street, Suite D420, Fremont, CA 94538) and to Mary Ann Segalla.

Contents

America
is another name
for opportunity.

—*Ralph Waldo Emerson*

A Word about
The Newest Americans

This series takes a look at the people who have been coming to America from 1965 to the present. It provides historical, social, political, and cultural information on the most recent immigrant groups that are changing the face of America.

Charts and graphs show how immigration has been affected over the years, both by changes in the U.S. laws and by events in the sending country. Unless otherwise noted, the term *immigrant* in this book, including the charts and graphs, refers to new legal immigrants and to refugees and asylees who have changed their status to legal permanent residents.

From its very beginning, the United States stood for opportunity and freedom. It exists because immigrants, people who moved from their homes to make a new life in a new country, dreamed of better lives. They dreamed of having a voice in their government, of expressing their opinions and practicing their religion without fear of being imprisoned or tortured. Two hundred years later, these dreams still call to people around the world.

opposite:
A recent immigrant to the United States, the popular singer and songwriter Shakira is a blend of nationalities. Her mother is Colombian, and her father was born in Lebanon.

An Immigrant Nation

America declared its independence from British rule in 1776. At that time, nearly 80 percent of the people living in the colonies were white Europeans from England, Ireland, Scotland, Germany, the Netherlands, France, and Sweden. Just over 20 percent were slaves from Africa, the one group of American immigrants who did not come to this country willingly.

Over the next 200 years, more than 70 million people from around the world would *immigrate* to the United States. The majority came for *economic* reasons, eager to make the American dream a reality. Although this was one of the largest migrations of people in history, it began slowly. Wars in the United States and Europe kept immigration to a minimum until the 1820s. As things became more settled, however, a rapidly growing population that had few opportunities in Europe looked once more to America.

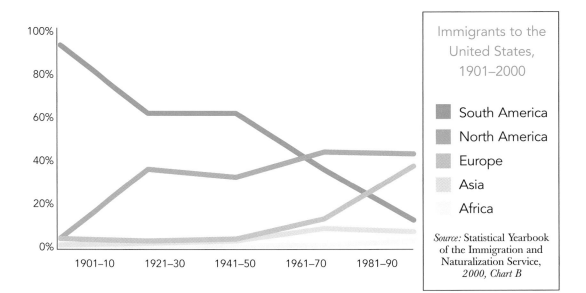

Immigrants to the United States, 1901–2000

- South America
- North America
- Europe
- Asia
- Africa

Source: Statistical Yearbook of the Immigration and Naturalization Service, *2000, Chart B*

Out of Many, One

—Motto of the United States

The 1800s

America offered freedom and political equality, but it also had practical attractions. Vast amounts of land unclaimed by white settlers, coupled with a growing number of jobs in the United States, exerted a strong pull on the imagination. Immigrants believed that they could improve their lives—and maybe even become wealthy—if they could only get to America.

There were many factors "pushing" immigrants to the United States as well. Population explosions, poor economic conditions, and widespread famine in Europe left many without work during the 1830s and 1840s.

The next big wave of immigrants reached American shores in the 1880s and 1890s. This time the newcomers included large numbers of southern and eastern Europeans. Immigrants from Italy, Austria-Hungary, Russia, and Poland began settling in America's cities and working in the factories.

The 1900s

Immigration to the United States set a record in the first decade of the twentieth century. Nearly 9 million immigrants were recorded as entering the United States from 1901 to 1910.

Immigrant Chains

Immigrant chains form when members of one immigrant family settle in America, and then convince family members and friends to join them. The established immigrants help the new immigrants find homes and work in the same area. Immigrant chains have influenced settlement patterns all over the country, helping to create large communities of Cubans in Miami, Dominicans in New York, and Chinese in San Francisco, among others.

For the first time, immigrants from southern and eastern Europe were in the majority. Many of these immigrants were Jewish and Catholic, in contrast to the predominantly Protestant groups that settled the United States. Immigration surged again from 1918 through 1921. Only when Congress enacted a quota system in 1921 and 1924 did immigration begin to decline. The *quota* system severely restricted the number of immigrants that would be allowed to enter the United States from each foreign country.

Immigration numbers remained low until the mid-1960s. But two events in particular caused America to rethink an immigration policy based on race and ethnicity. The first event was the *genocide* (systematic destruction) of European Jews during World War II. German leader Adolf Hitler's vision of a racially pure world was in direct opposition to the ideals the United States was based on. Yet the immigration policy was set up to admit primarily white Europeans. The second event was the American civil rights movement, which began in the mid-1950s and gained momentum in the 1960s. Many people felt that the United States, as a world leader, should adopt an immigration policy that would reflect its ideals of equality and freedom for everyone regardless of race or country of origin.

The Immigration and Nationality Act of 1965 introduced far-reaching changes in American immigration policy. The quota system was discarded in favor of worldwide limits. With family reunification as a priority, lawmakers allowed immediate family members of U.S. citizens to be admitted without limit.

Terrorist acts against the United States in 1993 and 2001 sparked changes to the immigration policy once again. The location of temporary (nonimmigrant) visitors, including students and businesspeople, is now being tracked more closely. The government has more freedom to investigate and detain suspected terrorists.

Immigration Today

In 2000, nearly 850,000 people became legal immigrants. Legal immigrants, also called legal permanent residents, receive paperwork, or documentation, that shows they are living in the United States legally. The documentation, commonly called a "green card," also allows a new permanent resident to work in the United States.

American immigration laws determine how many foreigners, or aliens, can enter the United States each year. Currently, the law allows between 421,000 and 675,000 immigrants to be admitted each year. Most of the yearly admissions are reserved for family-sponsored immigrants (up to 480,000 per year). People who have job skills that are in demand, such as scientists, software programmers, and computer analysts, are also among the first chosen. They qualify for the employment-based preferences (up to 140,000 per year).

Each year, 50,000 to 55,000 immigrants enter the United States through the Diversity Program. This program addresses the inequalities of past immigration policies. Residents of countries that have sent fewer than 50,000 immigrants to the United States in each of the past five years are eligible to participate. Visas, or permits, are issued to those applicants whose names are randomly selected, giving the program its common name—the diversity lottery.

Immigration Legislation

Until the late 1800s, there were few federal restrictions on immigration. States had the ability to control or limit immigration. This changed in 1875 when the federal government gained control of immigration. Beginning in the 1920s, the laws also specified the number of immigrants that could come to the United States each year.

Here is a brief description of the laws that have changed American immigration patterns over the past 200 years:

Immigrant Admissions in 2000

a	Immediate relative of U.S. citizen	41%
b	Family preference	28%
c	Employment preference	13%
d	Refugee/asylee adjustment	8%
e	Diversity Program	6%
f	Other	4%

Source: Immigration and Naturalization Service

1882 The *Chinese Exclusion Act* stopped nearly all new immigration from China. Chinese immigrants would not be admitted in large numbers again until the 1950s.

1907 The so-called *Gentlemen's Agreement* blocked most Japanese immigration. A presidential order kept Hawaiian Japanese from moving to the United States.

1917 The *1917 Immigration Act* required immigrants to pass a literacy test before entering the United States. It also created a zone covering most of Asia. No immigration from this zone was allowed.

1921   The *Quota Act* temporarily limited immigration after World War I. Immigration limits were based on national origin. Immigrants from the Western Hemisphere were not subject to limits.

1924   The *1924 Immigration Act* established the first permanent limits on immigration, continuing the national origins quota system. Before this law was enacted, the idea of illegal immigration did not exist.

1952   The *Immigration and Nationality Act of 1952* lifted some of the restrictions on Asian countries. Discrimination based on gender was eliminated. For the first time, preference was given to foreigners whose skills were in demand and to relatives of U.S. citizens and residents. Race-based limits were abolished when all races became eligible for naturalization.

1965   The groundbreaking *Immigration and Nationality Act of 1965* (also known as the Hart-Cellar Act) eliminated the quota system for worldwide limits.

1980   The *Refugee Act of 1980* established procedures for admitting and resettling *refugees*. It also made a distinction between refugees and asylees.

1986   The *Immigration Reform and Control Act (IRCA)* attempted to address the problem of illegal immigration. It provided an opportunity for immigrants who were living and working illegally in the United States before January 1, 1982, to adjust their status and eventually become legal residents and naturalized citizens.

1990   The *Immigration Act of 1990* made several major changes in U.S. policy. The total number of immigrants and refugees allowed to enter the United States each year increased dramatically. A Diversity Program allowed immigrants from countries that were underrepresented in America in the past an extra chance to receive a visa.

1996   The *Antiterrorism and Effective Death Penalty Act* outlined measures to identify and remove terrorists from the United States. It allowed the U.S. government to use evidence collected in secret to accuse immigrants of terrorist acts.

1996   The *Welfare Reform Act* was designed to keep most legal immigrants from getting food stamps and supplemental security income provided by the federal government.

1996   The *Illegal Immigration Reform and Immigrant Responsibility Act* focused on improving control of the U.S. borders.

2001   The *U.S.A. Patriot Act* expanded the government's ability to investigate, arrest, and deport legal residents for failing to comply with immigration regulations. Immigrants (including legal residents) who were suspected of terrorism could now be held indefinitely in detention centers.

Refugees and Asylees

Some people have to leave their countries because it isn't safe to live there anymore. Those who are afraid to return to their country because of persecution ask countries like the United States to take them in. People who are living outside the United States when they apply for protection are called refugees. They often have to wait years before their application is granted. The number of refugees permitted to resettle in the United States each year is determined by the president after discussions with Congress.

Like refugees, asylees are also seeking *asylum,* or safety from persecution. The difference is that asylees make their way to the United States before they ask for asylum. Most asylees come from countries that are located near the United States, such as Cuba, Nicaragua, and Guatemala.

Illegal Immigrants

In addition to the nearly 1 million legal immigrants who arrive in the United States each year, hundreds of thousands of people enter the country without permission. No one really knows how many illegal immigrants enter the United States each year. The Immigration and Naturalization Service (INS) estimates the number at close to 300,000 per year. These immigrants don't have the papers (visas) that show they have been admitted legally to the United States. They are often referred to as undocumented aliens or illegal immigrants.

In 1996, the INS estimated that 5 million undocumented immigrants were living in the United States. Today, experts suggest that the number is between 6 and 9 million. Over half are from Mexico. Because it is easier for people from nearby countries to enter the United States illegally, eight of the top ten countries sending illegal immigrants are in Central America, the Caribbean, and North America. The other two are the Philippines and Poland.

A group of new Americans take the oath of citizenship at Faneuil Hall in Boston.

Becoming Naturalized Citizens

American citizens enjoy many rights that permanent residents and visitors do not have. American citizens have the right to vote to select their leaders. They may hold government jobs and run for elected office. They can ask the government to allow family members to come to live in the United States. American citizens can also apply for a U.S. passport, making it easier to travel abroad.

Anyone who is born in the United States is automatically a citizen. Immigrants who want to become citizens must go through a process called naturalization. Before permanent residents can become naturalized citizens, they must live in the United States for a specified amount of time, usually three to five years. Once the residency requirement has been met, the resident must submit an application to the INS. A criminal check is completed during the application process.

The next step is an interview between the applicant and an INS officer. The ability to speak English is judged throughout the interview. Questions about the history and government of the United States test the immigrant's understanding of American civics. At the end of the interview, the officer either approves or denies the application for citizenship. An applicant who fails one of the tests may be given a second chance to pass the test.

Applicants who successfully complete the naturalization process attend a naturalization ceremony at which they swear an oath of allegiance to the United States. Each new citizen then receives a Certificate of Naturalization. Children under eighteen automatically become citizens when their parents take the oath of allegiance.

American Attitudes toward Immigration

Throughout America's history, immigrants have been both welcomed and feared. Negative attitudes toward immigrants tend to increase when the economy is in a slump. Increased competition for jobs and fears for the future lead many Americans to close ranks.

Discrimination

From the start, immigrants faced *discrimination* in America regardless of their race. Irish-Catholic, Japanese, Chinese, and Filipino immigrants have all been targets of hostility through the years.

Immigrants today continue to struggle to fit in. They are judged by their ability to speak English, their skin color, their clothing. Immigrant children comment that their new English vocabulary includes words like "discrimination," "prejudice," and "stereotype."

Immigration Myths and Realities

The debate over immigration has been heated from time to time. Amazingly, the same arguments against immigration have been made for over 100 years. Below are some of the claims that are often made about immigrants. The facts are also given.

Myth	*Reality*
Immigrants take jobs away from Americans.	New immigrants usually accept low-paying jobs that Americans don't want or won't accept. Immigrants often revitalize urban areas. Many open new businesses, providing jobs for others.
There are too many immigrants today. They outnumber Americans.	The actual number of immigrants in recent years does exceed that of past years. Immigrants in the 1990s, however, made up less than 3 percent of the population, compared to 9.6 percent from 1901 to 1910.
Immigrants come to America because they want to receive financial assistance, called welfare, from the government.	New immigrants must prove that they won't be a burden before they are allowed to enter the United States. Historically, new immigrants are more likely to be employed, save more of their earnings, and are more likely to start new businesses than native-born Americans. Recently, however, the percentage of immigrants receiving welfare is nearing that of native-born Americans.
Immigrants keep to themselves and speak their own languages. They don't want to be Americans.	Immigrants know that English is the key to success in the United States. Classes teaching English as a second language fill up quickly. There is usually a waiting list. Studies show that children of immigrants actually prefer English.
There is too much diversity among immigrants today. *Ethnic* enclaves, or communities, mean that immigrants don't have to adapt to the U.S. *culture*.	Some social scientists argue that *ethnic* enclaves form when immigration is not diverse enough.

The Immigrant Experience

Destinations

Allll immigrants to the United States have to make life-altering decisions that will change the course of their future. Their decisions are usually based on three main factors: location of family members, if any; opportunities for work; and proximity, or closeness, to their home country. These three factors have influenced settlement patterns since immigrants first began arriving on America's shores.

Although immigrants can live anywhere in the United States, nearly two-thirds of them settle in just six states. California, New York, Florida, Texas, New Jersey, and Illinois count more immigrants among their population than all other states combined. California alone is the destination of one-fourth of the nation's immigrants.

Because finding work and living near others who share their experience is so important, nearly all new immigrants (93 percent) live in urban areas. The most popular U.S. destinations in 2000 were New York City, Los Angeles, Miami, Chicago, and Washington, D.C.

Refugees do not necessarily follow these same settlement patterns, at least when they first arrive. As part of their relocation package, they are resettled into communities across the United States. Individuals or families in that community *sponsor* the refugees, helping them get used to their new surroundings. When refugees adjust their status to immigrant, they often choose to move to a location with a larger immigrant community.

Immigrant Destinations

a	California	25.6%
b	New York	12.5%
c	Florida	11.6%
d	Texas	7.5%
e	New Jersey	4.7%
f	Illinois	4.3%
g	All other states	33.8%

Source: Immigration and Naturalization Service

Fitting In

Social scientists call the process of adapting to a new culture *assimilation*. Assimilation takes place over time and in different ways. There is economic assimilation, in which immigrants take advantage of workplace opportunities to increase their income. Social and cultural assimilation take place as immigrants form friendships with Americans at school and at work. English skills improve and cultural traditions from their home country may be adapted. Young people especially become immersed in the American culture and begin to adopt those values. Finally, there is political assimilation. This occurs when immigrants choose to complete the naturalization process so their voices can be heard in their government.

CHAPTER ONE

Afghans

Afghanistan,

a country in Central Asia that is slightly larger than Texas, has been devastated by over twenty years of war. Millions of Afghans have left behind their homes, and sometimes their families, as they escaped from decades of foreign invasion, civil war and the harsh religious government called the Taliban (TAH-lee-bon), that came to power in 1996.

Many of these *refugees* made their way to the United States, where they still live today. The most recent wave of refugees to flee Afghanistan resulted from attacks against the United States in 2001. The attacks were carried out by groups of terrorists protected by the Afghan government. This led to the formation of a worldwide coalition to eradicate terrorism, starting with the *terrorists* hiding in Afghanistan. As a result, war continued and more refugees fled Afghanistan.

Today, Afghan Americans feel pulled in different directions. They know that the Taliban, who controlled Afghanistan at the time, harbored terrorists who have caused harm to the people of the United States. Afghans are united with other Americans in their grief over the destruction of the World Trade Center in New York City and the Pentagon on September 11, 2001. They agree that the terrorists who were behind this action ought to be caught and punished. However, they are keenly aware that the efforts by the United States and the coalition partners to topple the Afghan government and dismantle the groups operating out of Afghanistan have harmed innocent Afghan people. Many of those who have been injured or killed in the fighting were friends and family that were left behind. However, some Afghan *immigrants* also feel a sense of hope and opportunity, absent for many years, as they contemplate the possibility of returning to their homeland now that the Islamic *fundamentalist* government of the Taliban has been removed from power.

Reacting to the September 11 Attacks

The Afghan American community grieved with the rest of the country when thousands died in the September 11, 2001, terrorist attacks on the World Trade Center in New York City. Unlike other Americans, however, Afghan Americans faced the possibility of becoming victims themselves. Many were attacked or threatened by Americans who made no distinction between the terrorists and the Afghan people. Some Afghan Americans who maintained traditional dress stopped wearing turbans and head scarves in public. Others displayed the American flag in their place of business. Many Afghan Americans volunteered to act as translators for the government.

As weeks and months passed, evidence mounted that the terrorist organization behind the attacks was based in Afghanistan and protected by the Taliban. Afghan Americans had a new worry. Family and friends who had remained in Afghanistan were now in danger of becoming innocent victims in the United States' war on terrorism. But speaking out against the campaign in Afghanistan could be considered unpatriotic or might raise suspicion that the Afghan immigrants were siding with the terrorists.

For many, the struggle for identity—as a Muslim, an Afghan, an American—continues.

A Quick Look Back

Afghanistan is one of the oldest settled areas in the world, with evidence showing that humans moved into the area about 50,000 years ago. Its location on ancient trade routes brought many conquerors together, fighting for control of the valuable region.

Foreign invaders made Afghanistan a crossroads of many cultures. They influenced the region's language, art, and religion and established the many different ethnic groups that compete for power in Afghanistan today.

Afghanistan's Ethnic Groups

It is difficult to understand the history of Afghanistan without understanding the ethnic groups who fight for control of their country. There is much animosity between the ethnic groups and sometimes even between the tribes of the same ethnic group. After the Soviets withdrew, the hostility between the groups grew worse and they battled each other for control of Afghanistan.

Afghanistan's Ethnic Groups

a	Pashtun	44%
b	Tajik	25%
c	Hazara	10%
d	Uzbek	8%
e	Other	13%

Source: CIA
World Factbook, *2002*

The Pashtuns (Posh-toon) are Afghanistan's largest ethnic group, making up 44 percent of the population. Pashtuns live in every region of Afghanistan, although the biggest concentrations are in the agricultural areas in the south and east. They are Sunni (SOO-nee) Muslims. They speak Pashto, one of the two official languages of Afghanistan. Traditionally, Pashtuns have held most of the power in the government, although some of that power was lost when millions fled the country during the Soviet invasion. The Taliban government was predominantly Pashtun.

The next largest ethnic group is the Tajik (TAH-jeek), with about 25 percent of the population. Most Tajiks live in cities and towns, especially Herat (HER-rot) in western Afghanistan and the capital city of Kabul (KAH-bull). There is also a large concentration of ethnic Tajik in the mountainous areas of the northeast. The Tajik are predominantly Sunni Muslims. Their language, Dari (DAH-ree), is the second official language. Dari has always been the language of government and business. Most educated or wealthy Afghans are Tajik. They have a strong presence in government, business, schools, health care, and the arts. The Tajik are leaders of the Northern Alliance resistance movement.

The Turkic groups include the Uzbek (ooz-BEK) and Turkmen (TURK-mon). Together, they comprise about 11 percent of the population. They live in the northern plains region. They have their own Turkic languages, but most also speak Pashto or Dari as well.

Other smaller ethnic groups have traditionally allied themselves with the Pashtuns or the Tajiks. The Hazara (ha-ZAR-ra) are Shi'ite Muslim. They were victims of *genocide* during the reign of the Taliban.

The Afghan Empire

Many dynasties ruled over Afghanistan in the 2,000 years before the first Afghan Empire, or kingdom, was established. Amad Shah, chief of one of the Pashtun tribes, took control of Kabul in 1747. Under his rule, the Afghan Empire reached into India and Persia. Over the next centuries, the empire went through periods of weakness and growth, but remained under the control of Amad's descendants. In 1880, the current borders of Afghanistan were established. Although the resulting country did not include all of the territory claimed by the Afghan Empire, the new borders made the country easier to defend against Russian and British threats.

End of the Empire

In the early 1900s, the Afghan rulers took steps to modernize Afghanistan. Schools and businesses were the focus in the first decade. King Amanullah (1919–1929) carried reform further. He required men to wear Western-style clothing in public areas and women to abandon *burkas* (BURR-kahz), garments that covered them from head to toe. Outrage from religious and tribal leaders forced Amanullah to leave the country in 1929.

The next king, Muhammad Nadir Shah, brought stability back to Afghanistan within a year. His son, King Zahir Shah, took power when his father was assassinated in 1933. He led the kingdom through forty years of relative peace. His cousin, Daud, served as prime minister. He established ties with the Soviet Union, accepting military and economic aid that would help modernize the country. His efforts to modernize the country and give more rights to

The one-time king of Afghanistan, Mohammed Zahir Shah, shown in November 1987. Zahir Shah has been living in exile in a Roman villa since he was ousted in a 1973 coup.

women were supported by many professionals who lived in the cities, but rural religious leaders opposed them.

When King Zahir Shah tried to force Daud out of the government, Daud seized control and named himself president. He ruled as a *dictator*. Opposed by nearly every group in the country, he was overthrown by Communists in 1978. The new Communist president, Noor Mohammad Taraki, announced radical reforms, including more rights for women. The *mujahideen* (MOO-jah-hi-deen, Islamic guerrilla fighters), who favored a more conservative, traditional society, organized and began launching attacks against the government. Afghanistan quickly became unstable, with a weak and precarious leadership.

Soviet Invasion

An Afghan leads his mule between two Soviet tanks that guard the road between Kabul and Jalalabad in early 1980, shortly after the Soviet invasion of the country.

In December 1979, Soviet tanks rolled across Afghanistan's borders and took over the government. The Soviets claimed to be protecting their southern border from turmoil and upheaval by invading. They also said that they wanted to stop the spread of Islamic fundamentalism. But opponents of the Soviet Union point out that the Soviets were protecting a position that would put them closer to the Persian Gulf and its rich deposits of oil.

Tribal religious leaders declared holy war on the Soviets and organized mujahideen to fight against Soviet troops. The United States provided aid and weapons to the mujahideen to help them overthrow the Communists.

The Soviet Union occupied Afghanistan for nearly ten years. Repeated bombings destroyed village after village. Millions of Afghans fled, living as refugees in other countries. *Land mines* were planted in many fields and villages, where they remain today. Realizing that it was caught in an expensive war that seemed to have no end, the Soviet Union began removing its troops from Afghanistan in 1985. By the time the Soviets completed their withdrawal in 1989, nearly a million Afghans had been killed, along with almost 15,000 Soviet soldiers.

Civil War

The Soviet withdrawal did not bring peace to Afghanistan. Instead, fierce, bloody fighting became a fact of life for Afghans as the different mujahideen and tribal groups tried to gain control of the country. Afghanistan's capital city, Kabul, was nearly destroyed during the civil war. In 1992, two mujahideen groups joined Uzbek, Tajik, and Hazara fighters to form the Northern Alliance. When they gained control of the government, they barred the Pashtun leadership from holding most important offices. The Pashtuns fought to regain their power.

The Taliban, a predominantly Pashtun mujahideen army, took control of Kabul in 1996. After seventeen years of war, the Taliban seemed to bring a sense of calm to Kabul. Many Afghans were relieved and hopeful that peace would finally return.

The Taliban

The Taliban ruled Afghanistan through a strict interpretation of the religious laws of the Islamic holy book, the Qur'an (koo-RAHN). Movies, music, and sports were banned, as were white socks. Every man had to grow a beard and could be punished if it wasn't long enough. Men were forced to pray five times daily. Speaking out against the Taliban's policies invited severe punishment, torture, even death.

Although everyone's lives changed under the Taliban, women suffered the most. They were not allowed to leave their homes without a male escort. When they did appear in public, they were required to wear a burka. They were not allowed to attend school or to work. These rules were enforced under threat of death, even if the men in the family were off fighting in the war or had been killed. Many women were in an impossible situation: they could risk being killed by the Taliban for going to the market for food, or they could follow the Taliban law and watch their children starve to death in their homes.

Under the Taliban's rule, terrorist organizations that opposed the values of democracy and economic freedom in the United States and American foreign policy in the Middle East were allowed to grow and become powerful. Terrorists trained by a Taliban-backed organization, Al Qaeda, bombed two U.S. embassies in Africa in 1998 and a U.S. Navy ship in Yemen in 2000. After the World Trade Center and the Pentagon were attacked on September 11, 2001, however, an international coalition led by the United States moved in full force to root out and dismantle the Taliban and Al Qaeda groups. The Northern Alliance of Afghanistan, a small army of Afghans who fought against the Taliban, led the ground attack.

Interim Afghan leader Hamid Karzai talks to Afghan religious leaders in Kabul following the removal of the Taliban government from power.

Afghanistan Today

With the Taliban government now removed from power, an interim government, led by Hamid Karzai (HA-meed KAR-zuy), oversaw a committee to select tribal leaders and representatives to serve on a Loya Jirga, or Grand Assembly. This traditional tribal council, the first one in over forty years, selected Karzai, a well-respected Pashtun, to continue governing Afghanistan until a general election can take place, no later than 2004. An international security force is in place to support the new government.

The Bamiyan Buddhas

Before Islam was introduced in Afghanistan, the Bamiyan Valley was home to a large colony of Buddhist monks. Around the fourth and fifth centuries A.D., these monks carved two giant statues of Buddha, an Indian mystic and founder of Buddhism (BOO-dizm), into the side of the mountain that surrounded the valley. The seated Buddha was 125 feet (38 meters) tall. A standing Buddha was carved next. The standing Buddha was 175 feet (53 meters) tall—the tallest Buddha statue in the world.

After Islam was established in Afghanistan in the seventh century, religious leaders ordered that the hands and faces of the statues should be destroyed. Over a thousand years later, in 2001, the Taliban blew up what remained of the ancient giants in spite of protests by countries around the world, including other Islamic countries.

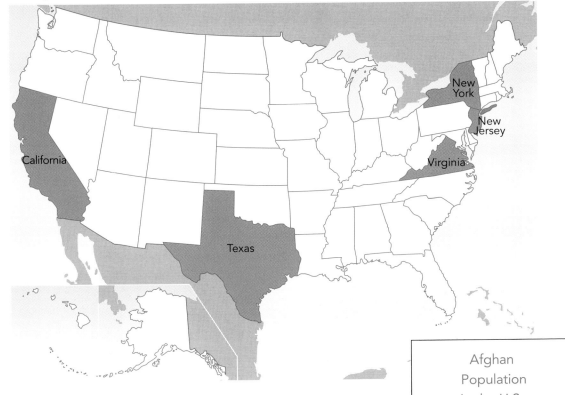

Coming to America

Afghan Population in the U.S.	
California	15,277
New York	5,829
Texas	3,772
Virginia	2,755
New Jersey	2,591

Source: U.S. Census, 2000

Many of the between 5 and 6 million Afghans found safety in another country during the Soviet occupation (1979–1989). Although many Afghans returned to their homes when the Soviets withdrew, others fled when civil war broke out in the early 1990s and during the Taliban's rule. Over 2 million Afghans lived in refugee camps during the 1990s. About a million more Afghans became refugees in 2001, when the United States announced its plans to wipe out the terrorist-based government camps in Afghanistan following attacks on the Pentagon and the World Trade Center.

Many refugees stayed in camps in Pakistan and Iran, but through the years, some made their way to the United States. Today, thousands

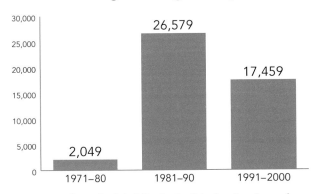

U.S./Afghan Immigration by Decade

Source: Statistical Yearbook of the Immigration and Naturalization Service

of Afghan Americans make their homes in communities across America. The majority live in the San Francisco Bay area of California, while the New York City area is home to the second largest Afghan American community.

Afghan Refugee Facts

People who leave their country to find safety in another country are called refugees. They face an uncertain life in refugee camps, where crowding and lack of food and medical supplies often create unhealthy conditions.

Source: Young Afghan-World Alliance (www.ya-wa.org)

• Afghans make up nearly one-third of the world's refugees, the largest single refugee population in the world.

• At the end of 2000, some 3.6 million Afghans were living as refugees.

• The United Nations High Commission for Refugees reported that more than 1.8 million refugees returned home in 2002.

The first refugees to leave Afghanistan during the Soviet invasion were rural families caught between the mujahideen and the Soviets. They sought safety in the refugee camps of Pakistan, Iran, and other surrounding countries. Many educated individuals and their families requested asylum from the United States. This group included government leaders and professionals, such as doctors and teachers.

Afghan refugee families wait to be given tents at the Mataky refugee camp near the Iranian border.

Spotlight on
DR. ZALMAY KHALILZAD

Afghan delegates talk with the U.S. special envoy for Afghanistan, Zalmay Khalilzad (center), outside the Grand Assembly, or Loya Jirga, in Kabul.

Dr. Zalmay Khalilzad (KAH-lil-zahd) was born in Mazar-I-Sharif (ma-ZEER-i-sha-REEF), a city in northern Afghanistan. As a high school student in Kabul, the capital of Afghanistan, he tried out for the national Afghan basketball team. Later he concentrated on his studies, completing a degree at the American University of Beirut in Lebanon in the 1970s. He then entered the graduate studies program at the University of Chicago in Illinois, where he earned his Ph.D. in 1979. Dr. Khalilzad remained in the United States, becoming a citizen in the early 1980s. Today, he serves as a presidential adviser and as the special presidential envoy for Afghanistan.

Dr. Khalilzad taught at Columbia University in New York City before being asked to join the State Department during the Reagan administration. Because of his knowledge of Afghanistan, he worked mostly on issues related to the Soviet occupation of his home country. During the presidency of George H.W. Bush (1989–1993), Khalilzad worked at the Pentagon helping to formulate America's defense policy. When George W. Bush took office in 2000, he chose Khalilzad to serve on the National Security Council, advising the president on matters in the Persian Gulf and Central Asia. In his role as special envoy, Khalilzad acts as a representative to the people of Afghanistan as they begin to rebuild their country and a new government.

Life in America

When Afghan families arrive in the United States they are confronted with a distinctive culture that is often at odds with their conservative way of life. Living in America often requires flexibility and a willingness to accept change and differences.

Family

When Afghan children arrive in America, they often feel pulled between their parents' world and their own. For instance, many Muslim girls are not allowed to wear makeup or date, although some secretly do both. Afghan boys occupy a position of importance in their home, but when they arrive in America their authority may be usurped by sisters who feel a sense of newfound independence. In Afghanistan, family ties and religion are very important. The extended family is very close and may share a house or a family compound. The oldest male makes the decisions for the family. When Afghan refugees come to America, they bring these values with them. Newly arrived immigrants, especially those who are over sixteen, are slower to adopt American culture than the young children. They don't understand why their children would want to attend college away from home or live in their own apartments, separate from the rest of the family.

Afghan Americans who were born in the United States and those who came here at a very young age grow up in a very American environment, one that encourages independence. The beliefs and values of their parents will never work for them. Often parents end up despairing that their culture and traditional way of life will be lost forever.

Work

As engineers, doctors, lawyers, filmmakers, artists, and entrepreneurs, Afghan Americans make many contributions to the American economy. Many early refugees were skilled professionals who continued in their field upon their arrival in America. For some Afghan refugees, though, arriving in America meant taking any job that was available while they learned the language and customs of their new home. Afghan American women are well represented in the workplace, often creating their own opportunities as they speak out for those women still in Afghanistan whose voices, until recently, had been silenced.

School

Afghans value the opportunities for education that they have found in America. Many of the Afghan children who arrived in the early 1980s are now college graduates, employed as engineers, doctors, lawyers, teachers, and business professionals. The majority of Afghan immigrant students, both boys and girls, attend public school, although some attend private Islamic schools in their communities. Because they were often denied an education in recent years in Afghanistan, women and girls are especially appreciative of the educational opportunities in America.

Afghan parents encourage their sons and daughters to study hard in school and prepare for a profession, especially in medicine, engineering, or law. While Afghan students complete all required coursework in coeducational classes, many Muslim girls feel more comfortable taking physical education classes in an all-female environment.

Most students adopt Western styles of clothing, although girls may cover their hair with a *hijab* (HE-job) in the Islamic tradition. (*Burkas* were imposed on Afghan women by the Taliban. They are not required by Islamic law and are not worn in America.) When girls first arrive in America, they may be stared at or teased. They don't realize that hijab are unusual here. Problems may arise when girls wear American clothes that their parents feel are too revealing; traditional Afghans value modesty.

In America, Afghan girls and boys are free to develop friendships with each other. They may play sports together and socialize outside their home—both activities were unavailable to them in their home country.

Religion

Nearly everyone in Afghanistan is Muslim, although beliefs vary depending upon which form of Islam people follow. Eighty percent of Afghans are Sunni Muslim; the remaining Muslims are Shi'ites. The Taliban, as well as leaders of the Al Qaeda terrorist group, follow a conservative version of Sunni Islam called Wahhabism.

Islam

Islam was founded in the seventh century by the Prophet Mohammad (MO-hom-mud). Muslims believe in only one god, Allah, the same god worshipped by Jews and Christians. Holy books, including the Torah, the Gospels, and the Qur'an, preserve the word of Allah.

Muslims believe that the following "five pillars of Islam" are the key to salvation:

• *Shahadah:* the acknowledgment that "there is no god but God and that Mohammad is the messenger of God"

• *Salah:* five daily ritual prayers

• *Zakat:* the giving of money to the poor

• *Sawm:* the dawn-to-dusk fast during Ramadan, Islam's most important religious holiday

• *Hajj:* the pilgrimage to Mecca, the birthplace of Mohammad

Forms of Islam

About 85 percent of the Islamic community follows Sunni Islam. The Sunnis believe that Mohammad died without appointing a spiritual successor.

Shi'ite (SHE-ite) Muslims believe that Mohammad appointed his cousin Ali and his descendants to be the spiritual and worldly leaders of Islam after Mohammad's death. About 15 percent of all Muslims follow Shia Islam.

Wahhabism is an extreme Islamic reform movement. Its members are the most conservative fundamentalist group in Islam. Members reject any modern interpretations of Islam. They label anyone who doesn't share their beliefs as infidels, or unbelievers, even moderate Sunnis and Shi'ites. The strict teachings of Wahhabism have been adopted by the Taliban in Afghanistan.

Muslim Texts

The Qur'an is the only holy book of the Islam faith. Muslims believe that the Qur'an contains the literal word of Allah, or God, which was revealed to the Prophet Mohammad. Memorizing and reciting these holy words is an important part of daily prayer and worship. (Many Americans refer to this book as the Koran, a Westernized spelling of Qur'an.)

While the Qur'an is the only holy text, there are other important books in the Islam faith. The Sunna is a collection of all the stories, sayings, and actions of Mohammad. Followers of Islam use these examples to determine what the Qur'an means. They often come up with different explanations, which is why beliefs vary from group to group. The Shariah describes rules for living a righteous life.

Major Religious Holidays

Ashura

The first ten days of the New Year are a period of mourning for the Shi'ite Muslims as they remember the killing of Hussein, grandson of the Prophet Mohammad in 680 A.D.

Ramadan

Ramadan (ROM-a-don) honors the time when Mohammad received the first of the Qur'an from Allah. It is the ninth and most holy month in the Islamic year. Muslims do not eat or drink from dawn until dusk during Ramadan. Instead, they reflect on their relationship with Allah, asking for forgiveness for their sins.

Eid al-Fitr

As Ramadan ends, Muslims gather with family and friends to celebrate the feast of Eid al-Fitr. Children often get new clothes for the holiday, which usually lasts about three days. Gifts are exchanged among friends and family.

Eid al-Adha

Eid al-Adha (The Feast of the Sacrifice) honors the prophet Abraham and his devotion to God. At the end of the hajj, the pilgrimage to Mecca, an animal is sacrificed, and the meat is divided between family members and the poor.

Holidays and Festivals

As families settle into their life in America, they often adopt American holidays while maintaining their own traditions. One tradition they do maintain is celebrating Nowruz, the Afghan New Year.

Observed on the first day of spring, Nowruz is a time for family and friends to gather and celebrate their blessings. Fish, rice, and sweets are served as symbols of new beginnings, success, and luck in the New Year. In some areas, Afghan Americans invite their community to share in the celebration of Nowruz.

Ramadan is also a tradition Afghans adhere to long after they arrive in America. More a religious observance than a celebration, Ramadan requires that Muslims fast every day for a month from dawn to dusk. (Pregnant women, the elderly, and the sick are exempted from fasting.) During this time, Muslims may visit the mosque every day to reflect upon their relationship with Allah. A huge feast occurs at the end of Ramadan where families and friends exchange gifts, make donations, and feed the poor.

The Arts

The ideas expressed by Afghanistan's musicians, painters, sculptors, and writers were often in conflict with the conservative government of the last decade, which wanted to control what the population believed. Many artists became refugees when the Soviets took over. Others left when the Taliban banned music and began destroying what was left of Afghanistan's art treasures. In America, these artists continue to express their love of their homeland through their art.

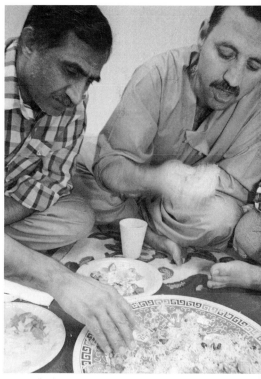

Afghan Americans break the month-long Ramadan fast with a feast of traditional Afghan foods.

Afghanistan has a strong tradition of storytelling. Afghan Americans have continued this tradition, sharing their stories and poetry through on-line magazines and Web sites as well as books.

Afghan artists living in America have continued to interpret their world through paintings and sculptures. Ahmanoolah Haiderzad, an Afghan sculptor who lives in New York, created a special coin recently. The Buddhas of Bamiyan

(BOM-i-yon), ancient sculptures destroyed by the Taliban, appear on one side of the coin. The other side features the twin towers of the World Trade Center, destroyed in the terrorist attack of September 11, 2001.

Many artists have expressed a wish to return to Afghanistan when it is safe, saying that art and music can help unite a country torn apart by decades of war.

Food

When Afghan families come to America, they are able to keep to their typical diet that includes flat bread called naan (non), soup, yogurt, vegetables, and fruit. Rice and meat dishes are also popular. Tea is a favorite drink. Muslims do not eat pork or drink alcohol. In most towns and cities where there is a substantial immigrant population, supermarkets stocking traditional spices and ingredients have opened.

Recipe

Naan (Afghan Bread)

Naan is the bread eaten each day by Afghans. It is usually formed into a long flat shape. On special occasions, black cumin or caraway seeds are sprinkled on top of the naan.

1-1/2 cups warm water (divided)

1 package dry yeast (1/4 ounce)

4 cups flour

1 tablespoon salt

1 tablespoon black cumin or caraway seeds (for special naan)

In Afghanistan, *naan*—small oval breads—are placed on the hot bricks of an Afghan oven to bake. In the United States, they are baked in a hot oven.

Preheat oven to 350°F. In a small bowl, dissolve the yeast in 1 cup of warm water. Put the flour in a large mixing bowl and sprinkle the salt over it. Make a well in the middle of the flour. Add the yeast mixture. Stir, adding the remainder of the water a little at a time until you have a soft, moist dough that can be handled easily. Turn onto a floured surface and knead until dough is smooth and elastic, about 5 minutes. Put dough ball back in bowl and cover with a towel. Let the dough rise for 1 hour.

Punch down the dough. Divide dough into 8 equal parts. Roll each part into a ball. On a clean, dry surface, pat each ball into an oval shape 6 to 7 inches long and 1 inch thick. Place the naan on an ungreased cookie sheet.

Make a decorative design on each naan using the tines of a fork. Sprinkle with black cumin or caraway seeds for special naan.

Bake for 20 to 25 minutes or until the top is brown. Makes 8 naan.

Source: Dr. Farid Younos

CHAPTER TWO

Cambodians

Cambodia,

a small country in southeastern Asia, is about the size of Oklahoma. The Cambodian people are from three main ethnic groups: the Khmer (k-may-er) or native Cambodians, the Vietnamese, and the Chinese. Throughout history, most Cambodians have lived in rural areas. The families there are generally poor. Farming and fishing are the main sources of food. There are few opportunities for children to attend school.

About 20 percent of the population lives in the towns and cities of Cambodia. Phnom Penh (pa-nom pen), the capital, is the largest city. People who live in the cities are more likely to be educated. French and English are commonly heard, as well as Khmer, the official language.

The Vietnam War shattered the Cambodian way of life in the 1960s. Hundreds of thousands of rural Cambodians fled to the cities and towns. The Cambodian army, which was very small, couldn't force the North Vietnamese who occupied their country out. To make matters worse, a group of Cambodian *Communists* called the Khmer Rouge launched their own fight against the Cambodian government. Their leader, Pol Pot, put in place one of the most brutal *regimes* (re-JEEMZ) the world has ever known. Torture, killings, and starvation by the government enslaved the nation.

Until the North Vietnamese Army invaded Cambodia in 1979 and gained control of the country, the world was not aware of the terrible conditions within Cambodia. The truth

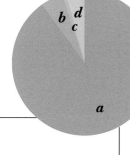

Cambodia's
Ethnic Groups

a Khmer   90%

b Vietnamese 5%

c Chinese   1%

d Other   4%

Source: CIA
World Factbook, *2001*

became known, however, as refugees who had experienced the horrors of the Khmer Rouge regime poured into Thailand. About half of those who survived the Khmer Rouge's reign of terror had lost at least one family member.

A Quick Look Back

Cambodia is an ancient land, home to the Khmer people. The Khmer kingdom of Funan (FOO-non) is one of the earliest known kingdoms. It grew and prospered between the first and sixth centuries. The cities of Funan established important trading centers linking India and China.

The most powerful Khmer kingdom, Angkor, was established in the ninth century. Over the next 600 years, the kings of Angkor built more than a thousand temples. The ruins still stand today, although the jungle hid them from view for hundreds of years. At its largest, the kingdom included what is today Cambodia and parts of Vietnam, Laos, Thailand, Myanmar (Burma), and Malay Peninsula.

French Indochina

For much of the 1800s, Cambodia was caught between its two powerful neighbors, Thailand and Vietnam. Bitter wars broke out, threatening to destroy Cambodia.

The Cambodian king turned to France for help in 1863. France had been establishing *colonies,* or settlements under French rule, in Indochina for several years. (*Indochina* is the name given to the peninsula between India and China. *French Indochina* refers to Cambodia, Laos, and Vietnam.)

France agreed to protect Cambodia. In exchange, France controlled most of the Cambodian government. During the ninety years of French rule, roads, ports, and rubber plantations were developed. For the most part, though, Cambodians continued to follow their traditional way of life.

After World War II, several groups throughout Indochina fought to gain independence from France. War broke out in Vietnam in 1946 as Communist and other forces fought against France. The war threatened to spread to Cambodia, but King Sihanouk (SEE-ah-nuk) was able to reach a deal with France. Cambodia was granted independence in 1953.

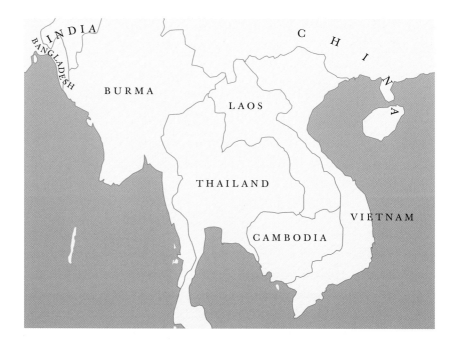

Vietnam War

Vietnam won independence from France a year after Cambodia, in 1954. But the peace agreement conditions set the stage for the Vietnam War, which started a few years later. Because of the Cold War, both the Soviet Union (USSR) and the United States had a special interest in Vietnam. The Soviet Union supported the *Communist* leaders in North Vietnam. The United States backed South Vietnam, which fought against the Communists. Because of its location, both the USSR and the United States wanted Cambodia on their side.

Cold War

The term "Cold War" describes the hostilities between Communist countries and capitalist, democratic countries following World War II. The United States wanted to keep Communism from spreading. The Soviet Union, on the other hand, supported Communist groups as they tried to force changes in their countries' governments. When Communists became active in a country, both the United States and the Soviet Union tried to influence the outcome by providing money, weapons, and other support. The Cold War ended in the 1980s when the United States and the Soviet Union agreed to stop the nuclear arms buildup. By 1991, the Soviet Union had dissolved. Today Russia and other former Soviet states are independent countries.

King Sihanouk kept Cambodia neutral for several years. In 1965, though, he let the North Vietnamese troops use Cambodia as a base for some of their operations. As the fighting got worse, many Cambodian villagers were killed. Cambodians began to protest against the North Vietnamese presence in their country. In 1969, Sihanouk and U.S. President Richard Nixon agreed that the United States would secretly bomb the North Vietnamese bases in Cambodia. Before long, thousands of Cambodian villagers were fleeing to the cities to escape the bombs.

The Khmer Rouge

In early 1970, Cambodia's Prime Minister, Lon Nol, took over the government while Sihanouk was out of the country. Under his leadership, the Cambodian army tried to force the North Vietnamese troops out of the country. At the same time, South Vietnam and the United States sent troops into Cambodia to find the North Vietnamese base camps. The Cambodian army, which was small and not very well equipped, was not successful in pushing the North Vietnamese out of Cambodia. Instead, many of the Cambodian soldiers were killed as the North Vietnamese moved deeper into Cambodia.

When the Khmer Rouge took control of Phnom Penh on April 17, 1975, most people were relieved. They thought that the Khmer Rouge government would bring peace to Cambodia. Instead, within hours of marching into Phnom Penh, the Khmer Rouge ordered the city emptied of its residents. Millions of people were moved to the country to work at government camps. In the process, families were torn apart.

Pol Pot and the Khmer Rouge wanted to make Cambodia a self-sufficient Communist country. Under their plan, Cambodia wouldn't have to buy anything from any other country. The government would own all the land. The people would plant and harvest rice and other crops. People would depend upon the government or "Angkar" for everything: food, information, even life itself.

The Khmer Rouge squashed every sign of education and intellectual life. Books, radios, newspapers, and religion were banned. Thousands of educated people, including doctors, teachers, and government workers, were executed immediately.

Speaking anything except the Khmer language, especially English or French, was cause for death as well. Even people who merely wore eyeglasses were suspected of being against the government and imprisoned or killed.

Starvation threatened the lives of those who were not executed. The small amount of rice each person was given each day was not enough to live on. Babies, children, and the elderly suffered greatly. People who couldn't work weren't given any food at all. People risked execution to search for food when the soldiers weren't looking. Snakes, bugs, birds: anything that helped them survive was a blessing.

Attacks along the Vietnamese border became common in 1977 as the Khmer Rouge tried to expand Cambodia's borders. Soon the Khmer Rouge was fighting a war with Vietnam. Within Cambodia, the Khmer Rouge began killing ethnic Vietnamese and Chinese citizens. Trying to destroy everyone within an ethnic group is called *genocide*.

In 1979, Vietnamese troops invaded Cambodia. Outnumbered, the Khmer Rouge forces retreated. Hundreds of thousands of people who had been forced to work in the government camps began making their way to Thailand. They hoped to find safety in the refugee camps there. Weak and malnourished, many died before completing the long trip.

Soldiers sit atop a tank on their way to join other Cambodians loyal to Pol Pot in the Khmer Rouge stronghold of Phnom Malai in northwestern Cambodia.

However, making it across the Thai border to the refugee camps didn't guarantee safety. Many of the Khmer Rouge soldiers posed as civilians in the refugee camps. They often stole the food and supplies that the United Nations and the Red Cross were sending to the camps.

Those who survived the Khmer Rouge refer to this time in Cambodia's history as *peal chur chat*—the sour and bitter time.

Vietnamese Rule

After Vietnam took control of Cambodia in 1979, life for those left behind improved in some ways. Schools were reopened. Buddhism, the religion of most Cambodians, was allowed again. People still had to work on the government farms, but conditions were much better. However, the new Cambodian leaders put into place by Vietnam still didn't allow freedom of speech.

> "When the war came into my country, it did not come in via the television screen, via the radio, via the newspaper. It came right into the streets. My war lasted three years, eight months, and twenty-one days. And every single day was a fight for survival. Every single day."
>
> —Loung Ung, author of *First They Killed My Father*

After fleeing the Vietnamese army, Pol Pot gathered his Khmer Rouge soldiers near the Thai border. Throughout the 1980s, they attacked the Vietnamese troops in Cambodia. The ongoing fighting, combined with harsh economic conditions, forced most to leave the country. Over a half million moved to the refugee camps in Thailand during this time.

By the end of the 1980s, Vietnam began to withdraw its troops from Cambodia. In 1991, the United Nations backed talks with all the groups fighting for control of Cambodia, including the Khmer Rouge. An agreement was reached that would allow the Cambodian groups to share power with a United Nations Transitional Authority in Cambodia (UNTAC) until elections could be held. After the agreement was signed, the UN began moving refugees from the Thai camps back into Cambodia.

Although it had signed the peace agreement, the Khmer Rouge continued its attacks on the population, turning the Cambodian army and UN peacekeepers against it.

Cambodia Today

The United Nations oversaw elections in 1993. Hun Sen, the leader at the time, did not win the election. He refused to give up his power completely, though. He pressured Prince Norodom Ranariddh, the elected prime minister, into sharing power with him and was named second prime minister.

In 1997, Hun Sen overthrew Prince Ranariddh and regained control of Cambodia, a move that stunned the rest of the world. He was reelected as prime minister in 1998, but many people questioned the fairness of the elections. When Ranariddh raised objections to the election results, negotiations resulted in a coalition in which each political party took control of different parts of the government.

Pol Pot's death in 1998 led to the surrender of many Khmer Rouge soldiers. Only a few have been arrested for their part in the genocide that took place under their leadership.

Coming to America

The refugees who escaped from Cambodia after the fall of Pol Pot and the Khmer Rouge faced a long stay at the camps in Thailand before being *resettled,* or moved to new homes in other countries. Since 1971, nearly 144,000 Cambodians have *immigrated* to the United States. Over two-thirds of these *immigrants* have settled in five states—California, Massachusetts, Washington, Pennsylvania, and Texas. The Los Angeles and San Francisco Bay areas have the largest Cambodian communities in California; Boston and Seattle are home to many Cambodians as well. In many cases, refugees went where the sponsors were available. Most others moved to areas where the climate was closer to that of Cambodia.

The first group of about 7,000 Cambodian refugees to arrive in the United States came between 1975 and 1978. They were primarily government or military leaders, citizens who were educated or

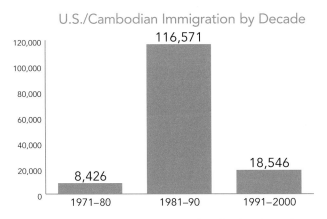

U.S./Cambodian Immigration by Decade

Source: Statistical Yearbook of the Immigration and Naturalization Service

wealthy, and those with ties to the United States. This group was fortunate enough to be able to leave the country just ahead of the Khmer Rouge's victory.

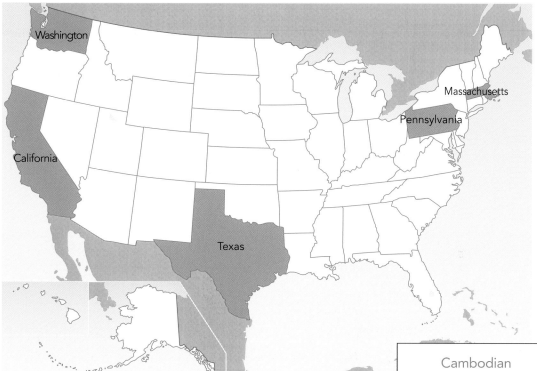

A second group of refugees settled in the United States in 1979. These 6,000 refugees had been able to escape from Cambodia before the Communist takeover as well. But they had been stranded in the Thai refugee camps for over three years.

About this same time, survivors of the Khmer Rouge regime began arriving in Thailand. About 134,000 of these survivors were granted refugee status in the United States between 1980 and 1992. Most of the refugees in the second and third groups had been raised in the rural areas of Cambodia. They were much less likely to be educated than the refugees who had arrived earlier.

Even after they arrived in the United States, most Cambodian refugees experienced severe depression and nightmares. They felt guilty for surviving when so many didn't. Many will never forget the horrors of the *peal chur chat*.

Cambodian Population in the U.S.	
California	70,232
Massachusetts	19,696
Washington	13,899
Pennsylvania	8,531
Texas	6,852

Source: U.S. Census, 2000

Spotlight on
DITH PRAN

Dith Pran and Sydney Schanberg are shown in this 1989 photograph.

One of the best known of Cambodia's refugees, Dith Pran, was the subject of the movie *The Killing Fields*. Born into a middle-class family in Phnom Penh, Dith Pran worked as an interpreter for an American military assistance group. He was also a receptionist for a British film crew and a tour guide. When the Khmer Rouge began fighting the Cambodian government in 1970, Dith Pran became a journalist. He wanted to tell the world about the war and the suffering of his people.

When Sydney H. Schanberg, a reporter for the *New York Times,* was assigned to cover the war in Cambodia, Dith Pran became his assistant. Over the next three years, the two worked in Cambodia and became good friends. When the Khmer Rouge forces approached Phnom Penh, Schanberg was able to arrange for Dith Pran's family to leave with the Americans. Schanberg and Dith Pran stayed to cover the fall of Phnom Penh.

Dith Pran, Schanberg, and other journalists were arrested when the Khmer Rouge took over Phnom Penh. The foreign journalists were allowed to leave the country. But Dith Pran was sent to the work camps with thousands of other Cambodians. He finally managed to sneak out of the country. When Schanberg heard that Dith Pran was in a Thai refugee camp, he flew to Thailand to bring him back to the United States.

Today, Dith Pran lives in the United States with his family. He runs the Dith Pran Holocaust Awareness Project. Its goal is to educate schoolchildren about the Cambodian *genocide* that occurred during the Khmer Rouge years. He also continues to work as a photojournalist for the *New York Times*.

Spotlight on
HAING NGOR

Born in a farming village in Cambodia, Haing Ngor studied hard and became a doctor with a successful practice. When the Khmer Rouge took control of Phnom Penh in 1975, Ngor was forced to leave the city. Because he was educated, he was put in prison, tortured, and forced to work in the fields. He watched as his family members were taken away to work camps or to be executed.

Dr. Haing Ngor used his fame and wealth to help other immigrants from Southeast Asia until his death in 1996.

After the fall of the Khmer Rouge, Ngor reached the refugee camps in Thailand and later immigrated to the United States. There he worked with other Asian refugees, helping them find work. A film director chose Ngor to be in a movie about the horrible things that had happened in Cambodia under the Khmer Rouge's rule. The film was called *The Killing Fields*. Ngor won an Oscar for Best Supporting Actor in 1984 for his portrayal of Dith Pran.

Even though he found success as an actor, Haing Ngor continued to help Southeast Asian refugees. He donated most of the money he made to support refugee groups. He often took medicine and supplies back to Cambodia to help the people who still lived there.

Haing Ngor died in 1996. He was found shot to death outside his apartment in Los Angeles, a victim of the gang violence and crime that were common in the area at the time.

Sichan Siv's experiences in Cambodia and his dedication to public service since immigrating to the United States made him an ideal member of the U.S. delegation to the United Nations Commission on Human Rights.

Spotlight on
SICHAN SIV

In early 1975, when the Khmer Rouge was approaching Phnom Penh, Sichan Siv was working there as an English teacher for a U.S. relief agency. This position almost guaranteed that he would be tortured or killed if the Khmer Rouge caught him when they reached the capital. In the weeks before Phnom Penh fell, the American government sent helicopters to take American citizens and relief workers to safety. When Sichan Siv missed the last helicopter, he tried to escape on his own. He rode his bicycle over 200 miles, but was captured just before he reached Thailand. He was taken to a work camp. A year later he tried to escape again. This time he made it across the border.

Officials in Thailand arrested Sichan Siv for entering their country illegally. The relief agency he had worked for helped him avoid those charges and arranged for him to *emigrate* to the United States as a refugee. He arrived in Connecticut in June 1976.

Once in America, Siv worked at odd jobs until he could attend college. After graduating, he worked at the Institute of International Education. He also served as an adviser to the Cambodian Delegation to the United Nations.

In the mid-1980s, Siv volunteered to work on George H.W. Bush's presidential campaign. After winning the election, President Bush invited Sichan Siv to become part of his administration. Siv was sworn in as a deputy assistant to the president in 1989. He was the first Asian refugee to become a ranking presidential aide.

Life in America

Primarily refugees and children of refugees, Cambodian Americans face many challenges as they struggle to make a new life in the United States. These people were forced to leave their homes to avoid being killed. They didn't have time to say good-bye. They may not know whether family members are still alive. They may not ever be able to return home. Their sadness may never disappear.

Family

Like most newcomers to America, Cambodians experience tension in their family life as they adjust to a new culture. A lack of time together, language difficulties and changing roles are all challenges for Cambodians who find themselves in a radically different world.

One of the biggest changes they encounter is the hurried nature of American society. Before the 1970s, life in Cambodia was quiet and calm, especially in the rural areas. Families spent a great deal of time together. In America, however, days are filled with work, school, chores, and English classes. Little time is available for everyone to spend together, although family members need each other more than ever.

Language differences cause problems for Cambodian families as well. Many older family members have trouble learning English. Part of the reason is that English is so different from Khmer, their native language. But they also remember a time when speaking English meant death at the hands of the Khmer Rouge. Children and youth, however, may speak little or no Khmer. Without communication, family bonds begin to collapse. Younger members of the family take on more responsibilities, including translating for adults. Parents may find themselves resorting to physical punishment—acceptable in Cambodia—when they are unable to communicate in any other way with their children. Unaware that American standards for discipline are different, they are sometimes reported to social services for child abuse because of this cultural difference.

In the traditional Cambodian family, a woman's primary responsibility was taking care of her children and her home. This included tending the gardens that provided food for each meal. She also helped raise the field crops, such as rice, that fed the family. In America, many Cambodian women are working in jobs outside the home for the first time.

Adding to these difficulties, many Cambodian refugees who lived through the killing fields suffer from post-traumatic stress disorder or other mental illness. They may have nightmares for the rest of their lives. Children often have to take on more responsibilities at home when their parents are suffering.

Work

Many of the Cambodians who survived the Khmer Rouge's murderous rule long enough to reach the refugee camps were unable to read or write their own language. When they arrived in the United States, they had difficulty learning to read and write in English, which made it hard to find well-paying jobs. Even today, many Cambodian Americans work in low-paying jobs that don't require strong language skills. Although Cambodians have lived in the United States for twenty years, many continue to live in poverty.

School

When Cambodian refugees began arriving in the United States in the 1980s, many of the children had never attended school. Life under the Khmer Rouge and in the refugee camps didn't allow for such a luxury. Going to school for the first time was a difficult adjustment for many children. They often found themselves in a school with few or no other Cambodians. Until they learned enough English to make friends, they felt very isolated. Even today, Cambodian American students often experience discrimination because of their differences. Teasing and taunting from classmates is an everyday experience for some. Often kids are farther behind in their studies than their American peers. They feel academically inferior and must work twice as hard to succeed. Some may have to attend summer school.

Religion

Cambodian culture is greatly influenced by Buddhist teachings. Most Cambodians are Buddhists and practice Theraveda (there-uh-VAY-duh) Buddhism, the most traditional form of Buddhism. A respect for all forms of life is at the core of their beliefs. There are relatively few Buddhists in the United States. Religious festivals and events are often held in rented places such as gymnasiums until the Buddhist community grows large enough to build and support a temple.

A small percentage of Cambodians are Roman Catholic or Muslim.

Buddhism

Buddhism is based on the teachings of Siddhartha Gautama, a prince in India who gave up his kingdom in order to seek the meaning of life. He became known as Buddha, the Enlightened One. Buddha taught that life is full of suffering, caused by desires. For instance, although the loss of a loved one grieves us, it is the desire to have the person nearby that causes us to suffer. Buddhism teaches that the only way to avoid this suffering is to reach an enlightened state—nirvana—in which we are free from the suffering caused by greed, hate, and ignorance. Buddha taught that people could reach nirvana by demonstrating love, compassion, and patience toward others and by living a simple life. These qualities are outlined in the Eightfold Path.

Buddhists believe that life is a continuous cycle of reincarnation—being reborn into a new life after our death. Buddhists try to live a better life than the previous one through meditation, honesty, good works, and nonviolence. Generosity, concern for others, loyalty to family, hard work, and honesty are also valued. These positive actions help a person accumulate good karma, or credit, which will help them be reincarnated into a better life. Fighting, drinking, and paying too much attention to money are considered immoral, and cause bad karma to build up. If one accumulates good karma in each successive life, one will eventually reach nirvana.

Holidays and Festivals

The Cambodian New Year is observed in April. It celebrates the growing season. In the United States, Cambodian New Year festivities generally last for one weekend rather than for two weeks as in Cambodia.

Celebrating the New Year in America

Buddhist monks offer prayers before lunch during the Cambodian New Year celebration at the Cowlitz County Exposition Center in Longview, Washington. The painted backdrop depicts the Angkor Wat temple in Siem Reap, Cambodia.

Cambodian Americans gather in the morning to celebrate the New Year with others in their community. If the community has a Buddhist temple, they meet there to pray and to meditate. If a temple is not available, families gather in a large meeting hall or gymnasium. Each family brings food to share and offerings for the altar.

Buddhist monks are seated at the altar. They bless the people and offer good wishes. People offer bags of uncooked rice as a gift to the monks and to the poor in the community. Surrounding the altar are offerings of favorite foods such as fruit, rice, and sodas. Incense and flowers are also placed on the altar as offerings.

The monks begin the ceremony by offering a prayer. At 11 a.m., they begin their meal. The families pray and chant as the monks eat. When the monks have finished, they invite the people to join the feast as they offer prayers. After the meal, dancers in traditional costume entertain the crowds. Many watch the dancers with satisfaction, knowing that this art form was almost lost when the Khmer Rouge killed nearly all of the classical dancers. Elders in the refugee community helped revive the art as they remembered the stories told through the dances. Each graceful movement was recalled until the dances were complete.

As the New Year's celebration winds down, people clean the inside of the pagoda and dust the statue of Buddha. Children apologize to their parents for anything they've done wrong in the previous year. Parents offer forgiveness and all try to lead a good life as another year begins.

Other than New Year's, it is difficult for Cambodian immigrants to celebrate their most important holidays in America, as most of their celebrations centered on the rural nature of their lives. The end of the rainy season marks the beginning of the busiest holiday season in Cambodia. Holidays, feasts, and weddings are celebrated from November until the Cambodian New Year celebration in April. Cambodians celebrate their freedom from French rule on November 9, Independence Day. The Water Festival, held in late November, recognizes the turn of the current of the Mekong River at the end of the rainy season. This holiday features many boat races. Once immigrants arrive here, they may not live near a body of water or be in step with the rhythms of agricultural life. They do, however, continue to schedule their most important family celebrations during this holiday season.

> "The suffering of Cambodia has been deep. From this suffering comes great compassion."
>
> —Monk's prayer at the New Year

The Arts

Across the United States, states and cities with large Cambodian communities have formed Cambodian American organizations. These organizations provide assistance in learning English, finding a job, and other critical, practical things. Many also preserve the Cambodian culture by providing lessons in traditional Khmer dance, music, history, and language.

Cambodian dancers demonstrate a native art form in Dance, Spirit of Cambodia *at the Joyce Theater in New York City.*

Food

Soup, rice, and fish are the main foods in the Cambodian diet. Rice is so important that the Khmer phrase that means "to eat" is literally translated as "to eat rice." Fish may be fresh or preserved, either fermented or smoked. Soups can be eaten at any meal, including breakfast. Desserts are not usually part of a Cambodian meal. Instead, sweet foods are eaten as snacks between meals.

A typical meal includes soup, salad, a meat or fish dish, vegetables, and rice. The dishes are generally served at the same time, rather than in courses. Hot peppers, herbs, and other seasonings are generally served on the side rather than cooked into a dish. Diners can then create a dish with the flavors and spiciness that they enjoy.

B'baw Mouan
(Essential Rice Soup)

4 quarts water

1 teaspoon salt

2 pounds chicken legs

2 cups jasmine rice

20 garlic cloves

1/2 cup plus 1 tablespoon vegetable oil

3 teaspoons fish sauce, plus more
  for serving

2 teaspoons sugar

1/2 teaspoon dried shrimp, rinsed and
drained

1/2 pound mung bean sprouts

4 scallions, thinly sliced on the diagonal

1/2 cup chopped fresh cilantro leaves
and stems

1/3 cup preserved cabbage

Lime wedges

Thinly sliced bird's eye chilies

Bring the water to a boil in a large soup pot. Add the salt and chicken. Return to a boil, then reduce the heat and simmer, partially covered, for 25 to 30 minutes or until the chicken is tender. Remove the chicken from the broth to cool.

While the chicken is cooking, rinse the rice under running water and drain.

Smash and coarsely chop 2 of the garlic cloves. In a large skillet, heat 1 tablespoon of the oil over high heat and sauté the chopped garlic for 5 to 10 seconds until golden brown. Add the rice, stirring to break up any clumps. Cook until the rice starts to brown slightly, 5 to 6 minutes.

Add the rice mixture to the broth and return to a boil. Lower the heat and simmer for 15 minutes, stirring occasionally. Add the fish sauce, sugar, and a pinch of salt and continue cooking and stirring for another 15 minutes, until the rice begins to get mushy, almost like a puree. (If the soup gets too thick, add more water.)

While the rice is cooking, coarsely chop the remaining 18 garlic cloves. Heat the remaining 1/2 cup oil in the skillet over medium-high heat. Fry the garlic until brown but not burned, 1 to 2 minutes. Remove the garlic with a slotted spoon and set aside.

Remove the skin from the cooled chicken, shred the meat with your fingers, and return it to the soup.

Put the fried garlic, dried shrimp, mung bean sprouts, scallions, cilantro, preserved cabbage, lime wedges, and sliced chili peppers on a platter. Serve the soup in one large serving bowl or four to six individual bowls. Add ingredients from the platter as desired. A common preparation is to stir the dried shrimp into the soup, add a handful of bean sprouts around the edge of the bowl, sprinkle the scallions and cilantro in the center, and top with fried garlic. Add the preserved cabbage, lime juice, and chilies to taste.

This popular dish is often eaten at breakfast. Serves 4 to 6.

Source: Adapted from The Elephant Walk Cookbook *by Longteine De Monteiro and Katherine Neustadt*

In rural Cambodian homes, there wasn't much kitchen furniture. Food was prepared on a clean cloth on the ground and usually cooked over an open fire. In the United States, young women usually prepare meals at the kitchen counter and use appliances such as microwaves or food processors. Some of the older women still prefer to prepare the food in a traditional way—on a cloth on the floor. Likewise, families may continue the tradition of eating meals while seated on the floor. Cambodian Americans who live in cities with large Asian populations can find the ingredients needed for most traditional dishes. Foods that are usually served in America, especially those made from cheese and other dairy products which are not part of the Cambodian diet, are hard for many Cambodians to get used to. If there are children in the household, though, their diet may begin to include foods such as pizza and spaghetti.

CHAPTER THREE

Chinese

China,

located in eastern Asia, is about the same size as the United States. It is one of the world's oldest civilizations. Hunter-gatherers first settled in the region around 10,000 B.C. They began to develop farming methods to support themselves, growing rice and other grains. Animals such as pigs, dogs, cattle, and sheep were domesticated as well.

China's recorded history reaches back 4,000 years. During that time, China experienced *rebellions, famine,* and political *regimes* that have led to widespread emigration. Some emigrants hoped for better economic opportunities. Others were escaping political persecution. Many made their way to the United States.

A Quick Look Back

opposite:
Four Chinese characters
engraved on a tombstone in
the Bigan Temple in
Weihui City are thought by
experts to have been
created by Confucius.

China is one of the world's most ancient civilizations. Archaeologists estimate that people grew grains and wove silk there as early as 5000 B.C. China was the most important country in eastern Asia in ancient times. Its influence on language, government, art, food, and philosophy is seen in many neighboring countries. As the centuries passed, the Chinese invented paper, printing, gunpowder, and magnetic compasses. China was considered one of the world's most advanced societies until the early twentieth century, when rebellion and *civil war* destroyed much of its progress.

Confucius

Kong Qui was a Chinese philosopher who lived from 551 to 479 B.C. His students called him K'ung-Fu-tzu, which means Master Kong. Westerners pronounced his name as Confucius (CON-fyu-shus), which is the name he is known by today.

Confucius taught that everyone had a role in society and that each role had specific duties. When people honored these duties, peace and prosperity followed. For instance, peasants were to obey their rulers and respect their authority. Rulers had the responsibility to govern the peasants wisely and to make sure their needs were met. These duties extended to parents and children and to husbands and wives.

The classic Confucian philosophy is detailed in a set of nine books. The Five Classics were written before Confucius's time. They include a collection of historical documents, ancient poetry, a description of rites and ceremonies, and a history of China from 700 B.C. until Confucius's death. The Four Books preserve the writings and teachings of Confucius and his followers.

Confucianism rose to prominence during the Han Dynasty (206 B.C.–A.D. 220). But as new dynasties emerged, teachings of Buddhism and Taoism (DOW-izm) mixed with Confucianism to form a new philosophy called neo-Confucianism (neo means "new").

The Chinese revolution in 1911 destroyed the dynasties and emphasized the state rather than the family. Confucianism lost its importance. The final blow to Confucianism came after the Communist victory in 1949. During the Cultural Revolution, Confucianism was criticized as backward-looking. Confucian teachers and scholars were treated with contempt.

While Confucian values did result in an orderly society, they reinforced a rigid class system. Generations of peasants remained poor because they were taught to believe that poverty was their fate. Education provided one of the few ways to improve their lives. Those rare young men who were able to teach themselves enough to pass the government tests were appointed to secure government jobs.

Although Confucianism may never regain the importance it once had in China, Confucian values are still ingrained in Chinese life today. Respect for elders, the importance of family, respect for hard work, and honesty are held in the highest regard by most Chinese. Education is still considered the key to advancement.

The Dynasties

From ancient times until the early 1900s, China was ruled by dynasties. A dynasty is a series of rulers who are from the same family. As wars were fought, states came under the control of one of the dynasties and their leader would become king. When the king died, his son or another male relative would become king. The earliest dynasties established a culture that valued family, obedience, and respect for authority.

The early dynasties also established a class system in the villages and towns they ruled over. The king's supporters, who were placed in charge of a state, became nobility, with their titles passing down through their family for generations. Below the nobility were officers, and below them, the peasants.

China saw constant fighting through the centuries, as one dynasty grew weak and a stronger one took control. Rebellion and famine marked some dynasties. Others were relatively peaceful, with advancements in farming and industry. Literature and the arts also flourished during the peaceful periods.

The population continued to grow, reaching over 400 million by the middle of the nineteenth century. As European traders and missionaries began coming to China, the peasants were exposed to another standard of living. Faced with floods, famine, and ongoing wars, they began to emigrate, or leave China, in search of opportunities. Most planned to earn money and then return home, but some ended up staying in their new locations permanently.

Rebellion

In 1911, the last Chinese dynasty was overthrown by rebels led by Dr. Sun Yat-sen. The Republic of China was formed and Yuan Shikai, a former army general, was elected president. Educational opportunities, especially for women and peasants, expanded. Western ideas gained acceptance. Magazines and newspapers encouraged the spread of new ideas.

While World War I was being fought in Europe, Japan tried to take control of China. Yuan refused to accept all of Japan's demands, but he did give up some Chinese land. After Yuan died in 1916, a series of military leaders (warlords) controlled China. China fought alongside the United States during World War I, hoping that the United States would then support China's attempts to resist Japan. When the United

States withdrew its support as part of the Allies' peace negotiations with Japan, the Chinese people grew angry. They protested the decision, not understanding how a country that supported independence could ignore Japan's ambitions to control China.

A strong base for a rebellion was being built during this time. Sun Yat-sen worked with the newly founded Chinese Communist Party, a group made up of the new Communist Party and former Chinese Nationalists. The Soviet Union provided assistance to the newly formed group that was struggling to win control of China. Although the Nationalists and the Communists cooperated at first, trouble soon surfaced. The root of the problem was philosophical: the Nationalist Party was made up of highly educated, wealthy individuals, while the Communists wanted China's wealth and land distributed equally. Distrust soon forced the Nationalists and the Communist Party apart.

The Nationalists gained control of China in 1927, but they were never able to build a strong, unified government. Many areas were still ruled by warlords or Communists. The Japanese were gradually taking over more land in the north.

The Chinese Communist Party, led by Mao Zedong (MAO zay-dong), reorganized in the rural areas. It launched *guerrilla* attacks on the Nationalists from its rural base. As Japan's invasions grew bolder, however, the Nationalists and the Communists joined together once more.

Mao Zedong is shown waving to a crowd at the beginning of the Cultural Revolution in 1966.

World War II

By 1938, the Nationalists and Communists were in a full war against Japan. Japan's forces were much stronger. They captured most of the northeastern territory, killing thousands of civilians in the process. When Japan attacked Pearl Harbor in 1941, the United States entered World War II and offered assistance to China's troops. The United States did most of the fighting against the Japanese, though. The Nationalists and Communists were too busy fighting each other. Mao spent much of the time building up the Red Army of the Communist Party with peasant volunteers. He put strict instructional and disciplinary techniques in place to foster the loyalty he would later need.

The Japanese surrendered in 1945, ending World War II. The Nationalist Party was supported by the United States. The Soviet Union supported the Chinese Communist Party (CCP) led by Mao. The Soviets gave the CCP the weapons surrendered by the Japanese.

The People's Republic of China

Civil war between the Nationalists and the CCP quickly broke out after World War II ended. By 1949, the Communists had won control of China. The Nationalists fled to safety in Taiwan, an island east of China. For over twenty years, the Nationalist government in Taiwan held the Chinese seat in the United Nations and was internationally recognized as the Chinese government. It was backed by the United States.

The Chinese Communist Party took control of mainland China, with Mao Zedong as its leader. The country's name was officially changed to the People's Republic of China. Initially, China formed an alliance with the Soviet Union, although the two countries later dissolved their relationship.

With the Communists in control, Chinese life began changing. Farms and factories were taken away from private owners and given to the state. Those who had fought against the Red Army were killed or sent to labor camps. Others, primarily wealthy or educated individuals, were criticized and humiliated in public. Children were encouraged to ignore their parents and teachers and to be loyal to the government instead.

About ten years after gaining control of China, Mao announced a policy called the Great Leap Forward. He wanted to show that, by working together, the Chinese people could create a strong industrial nation without the machinery used by Western nations. Rural peasants were organized into agricultural communes. Their small plots of land were combined into large fields. Backyard furnaces were built. These were meant to increase the production of steel without having to build factories.

The policy was a disaster. Party leaders who knew nothing about agriculture made decisions rather than relying on the peasants who knew how to farm. Crops were planted at the wrong time. Everything had to be sold to the government so there were no opportunities for real commerce. Mistakes like these led to the starvation of more than 20 million people from 1958 to 1962.

The Cultural Revolution

In the years after the Great Leap Forward, many people criticized Mao. People were still going hungry, and few had any opportunities to earn a living. Desperate to maintain control of China, in 1966 Mao announced a new plan he called the Cultural Revolution. Its stated purpose was to rid the country of bourgeois, or middle-class, ideals. But it would also allow Mao to eliminate people who disagreed with him.

University and high school students were encouraged to join groups called the Red Guards. Mao believed that young people, who naturally question traditional ideals, would aid his efforts to destroy old ideas, culture, customs, and habits. The Red Guards destroyed books, art, temples. They publicly accused adults, including their parents and teachers, of not being open to the new "Maoist" society. Educated people suffered the most. They were often put in prison, tortured, and starved until they admitted their "crimes" or until they died.

Students and teachers express approval of the Cultural Revolution with banners, photos of Mao, and shouts of "Long live Chairman Mao" during a 1966 rally.

Many were sent to labor camps where they were forced to work on farms. The only book they were permitted to read was *The Red Book of Chairman Mao,* an explanation of his rules and beliefs. The Cultural Revolution divided many families. Children and spouses were sent to locations thousands of miles apart to work for Mao and study his writings.

By the time that the Cultural Revolution finally came to an end, in 1976 when Mao died, it had disrupted the basic structure of Chinese society. The economy slowed. Young people had to put their education on hold. There were few books to study; most had been burned or otherwise destroyed.

China Today

Deng Xiaoping (DUNG SHOU-ping) gained control of the government soon after Mao's death. He began economic reforms in order to combat poverty. As part of his reform program, the People's Republic of China reached out to foreign countries. Industry was modernized with foreign technology. The government sought foreign investors for Chinese companies. The previous system of welfare states, in which people depended upon the government for jobs, ended. Farmers were given small plots of land and the opportunity to sell part of their crops at competitive rates. The government also placed restrictions on marriage and family in an effort to control China's rapidly increasing population.

As these reforms began to take effect, the United States became more open to the Communist government. By 1979, the United States had normalized relations with China. (The UN had recognized the People's Republic of China as the official government in 1971.)

Aside from economic reforms, Deng allowed more freedom of the press. The spread of television in the 1980s introduced many Chinese citizens to Western culture. American and European music and clothing became popular. People began to demand a better standard of living.

But despite all these reforms, China remained a Communist country with little tolerance for free speech. In April 1989, students gathered in Tiananmen Square in China's capital, Beijing, to hold a memorial for a government official who had supported their "Democracy Wall" movement that pushed for greater freedom and democracy in China. The memorial grew into an ongoing protest, with the students asking for a more democratic government with freedom of the press and less political corruption. The protesters also spoke out against Deng. The protest gathered strength when Mikhail Gorbachev, the leader of the Soviet Union, visited Beijing in May. Martial law was declared in late May, but the students continued their protest. The government silenced the protest on June 3 and 4 by killing hundreds of unarmed students and workers. Over 10,000 more were wounded. Many supporters were arrested and several were executed. People around the world were outraged at the violent suppression of the protesters. Many countries condemned the action.

Jiang Zemin was chosen as China's leader after Deng's death in 1997. The economy grew stronger, although inflation rose as well, causing higher prices for most goods. By the late 1990s, China had a strong, positive presence in the international community. Hong Kong, which had been under British control since the 1840s, was returned to Chinese rule in 1997. Likewise, Portugal released control of the island of Macao (ME-cow) in 1999. The United States and China signed a trade agreement in 1999, leading to China's being accepted as a member of the World Trade Organization in 2001.

Thousands of Chinese citizens pack Tiananmen Square alongside huge floats as the country celebrated fifty years of Communist rule in 1999.

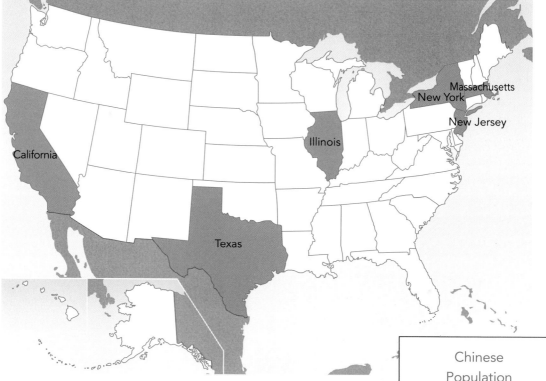

California
New York
Massachusetts
New Jersey
Illinois
Texas

Chinese Population in the U.S.	
California	959,871
New York	380,218
New Jersey	96,283
Texas	93,949
Massachusetts	70,634
Illinois	6,852

Source: U.S. Census, 2000

Coming to America

To day, over 2.3 million people of Chinese ancestry are living in the United States. Some belong to families that arrived in America over 150 years ago. Others are recent newcomers to our country. Most Chinese immigrants and their descendants have settled in California. But New York City is the top metropolitan destination.

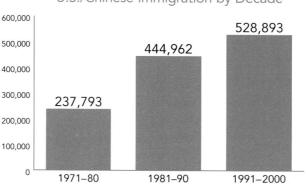

U.S./Chinese Immigration by Decade

528,893 (1991–2000)
444,962 (1981–90)
237,793 (1971–80)

Notes: Totals include both China and Hong Kong immigrants. Beginning in 1957, China includes Taiwan. As of January 1, 1979, the United States has recognized the People's Republic of China.

Source: Statistical Yearbook of the Immigration and Naturalization Service

Gold Mountain

Some of the earliest Chinese immigrants came to America to hunt for gold during the California Gold Rush of 1849. They dreamed of finding gold in Gam Saam—the Gold Mountain (California)—and returning to their country with enough money to buy land or establish a business. Instead, many immigrants found themselves working long hours at low pay. They were the targets of racial discrimination and hatred at a time when there was little law enforcement at all, let alone protection of the rights of minorities.

When Chinese immigrants first arrived, they were welcomed. Although many searched for gold, others started restaurants, laundries, or worked as servants and laborers. The borax mines in California and the Arizona copper mines hired Chinese workers. Many found employment with the railroad companies. Working first on railroads within California, they were later hired by the Central Pacific Railroad Company, which was created to build the western half of the Transcontinental Railroad, a railroad that linked the eastern and western coasts of the United States. Needing thousands of workers, the company began recruiting in China, hiring the first Chinese rail workers in 1865. About two-thirds of the railroad's workers were Chinese. In 1869, as the Central Pacific and Union Pacific Railroads drew close together, a Chinese crew was chosen to lay the final ten miles of track.

Coolies

Chinese laborers were often called *coolies*. The word came from the Chinese words *koo* (to rent) and *lee* (muscle). Together, they refer to a laborer, someone who rents his muscles.

As the Gold Rush subsided, unemployment soared. Resentment grew against the Chinese and other foreigners who had flocked to the area when gold was discovered. The Chinese were the target of most of the hard feelings. Their appearance, style of dress, and language quickly identified them as different. More importantly, the Chinese seemed to be successful when most men were struggling to find work. Many of those criticizing the Chinese were themselves immigrants from Europe.

Activists walk to the grave of Vincent Chin on the twentieth anniversary of his death. Chin was killed in 1982 in an act of racially motivated violence.

Racism and Hatred

Although Chinese workers experienced discrimination wherever they lived, the situation was particularly harsh in California. Over a hundred laws were passed, ranging from harassment to the denial of basic rights. Regulations limited the number of people who could live in one house or apartment. One law declared that Chinese, as people of color, could not testify in a court of law for or against a white person. This ban effectively took away any protection that our justice system might have provided. At the same time, groups promoting the removal of all Chinese from America were gaining membership.

The most horrible instance of racially motivated crimes against Chinese immigrants took place during the Chinatown Massacre in Los Angeles in 1871. A white deputy sheriff was accidentally killed during a fight between two Chinese men. Over 500 people converged on the Chinese community, looting stores and beating and killing Chinese immigrants. By the time order was restored, nineteen men and boys had been hanged.

Discrimination was not found just at the state level. The federal government ruled that Chinese were persons of color just like African Americans and Native Americans and therefore not allowed to become naturalized citizens. In 1882, the first immigration policy to exclude immigrants based on race alone became law. The Chinese Exclusion Act effectively shut down immigration from China until the 1950s.

Despite the hardships and prejudice, many Chinese did achieve success in the United States. They used the legal system to fight the discriminatory laws that had been passed, and they lobbied for the right to become citizens. They published rebuttals to arguments made by the anti-Chinese groups. The Declaration of Independence and the Constitution served as a basis for their belief that they should be treated fairly. Family associations and mutual aid organizations were established to provide support and protection to their members.

Prejudice and the related need for protection led to the growth of Chinese communities, called Chinatowns, within large cities. The Chinatown settlements allowed Chinese immigrants to socialize with others who shared their language and customs. The communities also offered some relief from the prejudice that the Chinese immigrants encountered. Today, the Chinatowns in large urban areas serve the same purpose for America's newest immigrants from China.

Chinese Immigration Today

In 2000, almost 70 percent of the immigrants from China entered under the family reunification programs for legal residents and citizens. About 30 percent came as part of the employment preferences program. China and the Philippines are the only two countries that have a waiting list for skilled workers who want to *emigrate* to the United States.

Instant Citizens

Some Chinese living in San Francisco during the 1906 earthquake had a unique opportunity to become citizens. During the earthquake, the building holding the birth records for San Francisco was destroyed. Hundreds of Chinese immigrants applied for "replacement" birth certificates. These certificates, listing the place of birth as San Francisco, would make them citizens immediately. County officials ruled that if a believable witness, such as the applicant's mother, was presented, the birth certificate would be issued. With Chinese women in short supply, one woman would pose as "mother" to many men. Overnight, many in the Chinese community became proud U.S. citizens.

An increasing number of Chinese immigrants are arriving in the United States illegally. They pay thousands of dollars to be smuggled into the country. Some arrive hidden inside container ships, large boats used to ship goods over long distances. Others enter the United States as members of group tours and then slip away. Entering Mexico or Canada and then crossing the border into the United States is another possibility.

The new arrivals—legal or illegal—usually make their way to large urban areas such as New York City, San Francisco, or Los Angeles. There they have a better chance of finding work that doesn't require special skills or knowledge of English. The Chinatown communities in these cities offer a place where the immigrants can adjust to life in the United States while maintaining their heritage.

Snakeheads

Like many countries, China has more people who want to emigrate to the United States than are allowed by U.S. law. Some of those who don't want to wait for a visa try to enter the United States illegally. Smugglers, called snakeheads, charge as much as $35,000 per person for an attempt. There is no guarantee that they will succeed; if the immigrants are caught at the border and sent back to China, they still owe the snakeheads money.

The majority of the immigrants who pay the snakeheads don't have enough money to pay the entire cost up front. These immigrants make a payment before the trip. Then they agree to pay a certain amount each week once they find work in the United States. It can take years to pay off the snakehead. During that time, the immigrant is vulnerable to exploitation.

Life in America

Chinese immigrants have been coming to the United States for nearly 200 years. During that time, many elements of their culture, including food and holidays, have been blended into American life. Although many Chinese American families have been in the United States for several generations, they often have to confront prejudice from people who still consider them foreigners. This has led many Chinese Americans to turn to Chinatown associations or to their neighbors for economic and social support, reinforcing the stereotype that the Chinese don't fully participate in American society.

Family

Family is everything to the Chinese. Confucian philosophy teaches that children should honor, respect, and obey their parents. In turn, parents are supposed to provide loving care and discipline to their children. Families are to honor their ancestors, whose spirits will then be happy and provide good fortune for the family. While many Chinese Americans still embrace these values, they also value the self-reliance and independence that is part of the American culture they've grown up in.

Work

The traditional values of working hard and obtaining an education have helped most Chinese Americans achieve success in the United States. Chinese Americans are well represented in the professional and technical fields. They also have a strong tradition of starting their own businesses, including computer-related enterprises, restaurants, markets, import/export shops, real estate companies, florist shops, and gas stations.

Chinese immigrants have been coming to the United States for nearly 200 years. They have incorporated their strong family values into their lives in America.

The biggest factor predicting economic success for Chinese immigrants is the amount of time they have been in America. Those who have just arrived often have to take low-paying jobs while they are adjusting to a new culture and learning a new language. Once established, however, they do quite well.

Like other undocumented workers, those who enter the country illegally often work long hours in low-paying factory jobs. For many, the sacrifice is worthwhile to provide their children with access to increased opportunity.

School

Chinese culture highly values education. Influenced over hundreds of years by the philosophies of Confucius, Chinese immigrants understand that a good education is one of the few ways a person can get ahead. But not all Chinese children are able to attend school as soon as they arrive in America. Often they will work illegally in a factory up to ten hours a day until their parents can find employment. Once they get to school, their studies become everything to them. They may feel that American students squander their time in school by paying little attention to academics and more time to socializing. Most kids who emigrate from China can't believe the amount of educational freedom America provides. When they go to a bookstore and read through books that would never have been available in China, students don't want to return to their home country.

Religion

The Chinese Community Church introduced many Chinese immigrants to Christianity when they arrived in America. The church provided a place where new immigrants could socialize with other Chinese. In many areas, it also provided English classes and social services. Today, the Chinese Community Church still welcomes new immigrants, but offers Chinese language and heritage classes to second- and third-generation Chinese Americans.

The Chinese have been influenced by many philosophies and religions over the centuries, including Buddhism, Confucianism, Taoism, Islam, and Christianity. Ancestor worship, while not an organized religion, has been a part of Chinese life for thousands of years. It is not unusual for Chinese persons to form their beliefs and values by combining elements from several different religions and philosophies, and continue to practice them in America.

Buddhism began to spread through China in the fifth century A.D. During the Tang Dynasty (A.D. 618–907), Buddhism was part of daily life for many Chinese. Judaism, Christianity, and Islam reached China during the Tang Dynasty, but they weren't as widely accepted as Buddhism. Jesuit missionaries from Europe arrived in China in the 1500s, soon after the first European traders.

Confucianism and Taoism are philosophies rather than religions. Neither promotes belief in an all-powerful god or life after death. Instead, they offer life lessons to help people lead rich and meaningful lives. Confucius emphasized respect for ancestors, authority, and education. Taoism teaches that individuals should live in harmony with nature in order to achieve happiness and a long life. Taoists avoid confrontation.

Organized religion was officially banned when the Chinese Communist Party took control of the country in 1949. After Mao's death, however, the government relaxed its stance. The practice of religion, as well as the right to remain an atheist, was supported in the 1978 constitution. Freedom of religion was restored in the 1982 constitution. However, the government didn't recognize all religions as legitimate. Some Buddhists and Muslims are still viewed with suspicion.

Holidays and Festivals

Traditional Chinese holidays are based on the lunar calendar, so their actual dates vary from year to year. The best known of the Chinese holidays is the Chinese New Year, celebrated in many cities across the United States.

Chinese New Year

The Chinese New Year celebrates new beginnings and family ties. It is one of the most elaborate and important of the traditional Chinese holidays. The Chinese New Year is celebrated on the First Moon of the lunar calendar. This typically falls between January 21 and February 19. Traditionally, the holiday lasts fifteen days, but in the United States it is generally adapted to fit into evenings and the weekend.

Before the New Year, families clean their homes thoroughly to sweep away any bad luck that has accumulated in the past year and make room for good luck. Cleaning is not allowed on New Year's Day to avoid sweeping any good luck out the door. Doors and windows are decorated with intricate paper cutouts and red banners called couplets that proclaim

Did you know?

The Chinese consider the seventh day of the New Year to be everyone's birthday. No matter when you were born, you would add a year to your age on this day. Chinese Americans generally follow the American tradition of counting and celebrating birthdays on the actual day they were born.

wishes for happiness, wealth, and long life. Food for the New Year's feast is prepared in advance. Then knives, scissors, and other sharp objects are put away to avoid cutting the luck of the New Year.

On New Year's Eve, the immediate family gathers for a feast. A place is set for every family member, even for those who can't be present. Foods are chosen for their symbolic meaning. The Cantonese, for instance, always serve fish on New Year's Eve. The Cantonese word for "fish"—*yu*—sounds like the word for "wish." It also sounds like the word for "abundance." The fish is served whole, with its head and tail on, to represent a happy beginning and ending for the New Year. Following the meal, some families keep the lights on all night long. They may shoot off fireworks at midnight to celebrate the New Year's arrival.

On New Year's morning, children receive *lysee*—gifts of money wrapped in red paper envelopes—and tangerines from their parents. (Red is a color of good luck and happiness. Tangerines represent good luck and riches.) Adults and children dress in their best clothes and spend the day visiting with

Scores of onlookers are treated to a performance of the Lion Dance in celebration of the Chinese New Year in New York City.

family. The visits to family and friends continue over the next two weeks. The purpose of these visits is to cast away old grudges and start the year with friendliness. Traditionally, no negative words can be spoken because they would bring bad luck. Any old debts must be paid off before the New Year begins. These customs continue today in many Chinese American families, although the visits to friends and relatives may take place in the evenings after work rather than during the day.

The New Year's Day meal usually features Jai, a vegetarian dish that all Buddhists must eat on New Year's Day. Traditionally, the dish had eighteen ingredients, each with its own meaning. According to Buddhist teachings, the first day of the lunar year is a day of purification. In order to receive blessings, no chicken, fish, or livestock can be killed on that day. The evening meal is usually served at home. Leftover dishes from the New Year's Eve dinner symbolize the abundance of the old year being carried into the new one. Stir-fried vegetable dishes, rice, and soup are also commonly served at this meal.

Chinese Americans don't always follow all of their parents' traditions at the New Year. Even when they do adopt some of the traditions, they may not believe the superstitions that accompany them. For example, if the tail of the New Year's Eve fish falls off while it's being turned, they don't necessarily believe that the year will be filled with bad luck. Most of the younger generation do still exchange oranges, tangerines, and lysee with their family and friends.

Traditionally, the Lantern Festival marked the fifteenth and final day of the New Year celebration. Lanterns were carried in a parade, and young men performed lion and dragon dances. Today, the Lantern Festival events have been incorporated into the parades sponsored by Chinatowns across the United States. The traditional lion and dragon dances are performed. Elements from a typical American parade, such as floats, marching bands, and beauty pageant winners, are part of the festivities as well.

Chinese Memorial Day

Ching Ming, the Chinese Memorial Day or Grave-Sweeping Day, is a spring festival. Typically held in early April, it originally marked the beginning of outdoor activities and the planting season. In ancient times, people held picnics with dancing and singing to celebrate this day. Colored boiled eggs were broken to symbolize life opening up. Today, the festival has become a time to honor family members who have died. The Chinese also use this time to reflect on their own lives as they grow older.

Families visit the graves of loved ones to clear away any weeds and to sweep away the dirt. They bring flowers to decorate the graves and incense to burn. Imitation paper money known as "spirit money" is burned so the dead will have money to spend in the afterlife. Firecrackers may be lit to scare off evil spirits. The noise also serves to let the deceased relatives know that their family has arrived to pay its respects.

Food is also brought to share with the spirits of family members. Whole roasted pigs, whole chickens, and whole fish are typical, as are dim sum and sweets. Bowls of rice, chopsticks, and cups of tea are set out. Each person bows to the graves. Then a sip of tea, and sometimes wine or whiskey, is poured into the ground near each grave.

New spouses or babies are introduced to the family spirits. Family members may ask the spirits of their deceased parents or grandparents to watch over them and provide good fortune in their jobs or lives. Families usually end the celebration by feasting on the food that they have brought, either at the cemetery or at the nearest relative's house.

Meaningful Foods

Cantonese families may serve some or all of these foods during their New Year's Eve dinner because of their favorable meanings. Traditionally, eight or nine courses are served because both numbers have lucky meanings.

Food	Meaning
Whole chicken	Wholeness of life on earth, a happy beginning and ending to the New Year
Clams, scallops	Wealth, prosperity
Roast pig	Purification, peace
Oysters, lettuce	Good luck, wealth, success
Long-grain rice	Long life
Whole fish	A happy marriage with many children, abundance, good wishes, a happy beginning and ending to the New Year. Fish is traditionally the last course to be served. Some should be left at the end of the meal. These extras are eaten on New Year's Day so that the upcoming year will be plentiful.

Mid-Autumn Moon Festival

The Mid-Autumn Moon Festival is similar in some ways to the American Thanksgiving. In the fall, family and friends join together to give thanks for a bountiful harvest and to hope for abundance in the future. Traditionally, the Mid-Autumn Moon Festival was held outdoors where people could admire the moon. Today, families often gather at parks or at home to enjoy the full moon and count blessings.

Moon cakes are the traditional treat for this holiday. Made in a special mold, moon cakes have a thin pastry layer enclosing a filling made of sweetened lotus seed paste or black bean paste. A preserved egg yolk is placed in the center. When the cake is cut into quarters, a bit of the yolk is seen. Most families purchase the cakes at Chinese bakeries since they are considered too time-consuming or difficult to make at home.

Some Chinese American children remember the other special treats that parents also purchase in the bakeries at this time. Cookies in the shape of Buddha are sold only at Moon Festival time. They have a loop of red string at the top so the cookie can be hung from the wrist or a shirt button.

The Arts

Chinese immigrants bring their love of art and culture with them when they come to America. No Chinese child is considered well educated without an understanding and appreciation for the arts. China is the birthplace of paper and printing, so it's not surprising that people there have been writing longer than anywhere else in the world. Some books were written as early as 3,000 years ago.

Did you know?

One Chinese legend tells how the moon cakes helped start a revolution. In the thirteenth century, foreigners from Mongolia invaded China. They ruled China as the Yuan Dynasty. The Chinese did not like being ruled by the foreigners and planned a rebellion. One of the rebel leaders got permission to give his friends gifts that honored the long life of the emperor. These gifts were the round moon cakes. Secret messages containing plans for the revolt were placed inside the moon cakes and delivered to villagers who would help overthrow the foreigners. The rebellion was successful, and the Yuan Dynasty was destroyed.

Jade carving, ceramic and porcelain work, silk weaving, calligraphy, watercolor painting, and sculpture are all highly regarded art forms in China. Many American-born Chinese children spend time after school practicing these arts in special classes or learning from their elder family members.

Spotlight on
IEOH MING (I.M.) PEI

The steel and glass Rock and Roll Hall of Fame in Cleveland was designed by I.M. Pei.

Ieoh Ming (I.M.) Pei (PAY), a Chinese-born architect, is one of the most influential architects in the world today. He has designed nearly fifty buildings in the United States, and more than half have won awards for excellence in design. Pei has also designed buildings in other countries, including the glass pyramid that serves as the entrance to the Louvre Museum in Paris.

Born in Canton, China, in 1917, Pei came to the United States to study architecture at Harvard. During World War II, he volunteered to help the National Defense Research Committee, a group of scientists conducting nuclear research. After the war ended, Pei returned to Harvard and completed his Master of Architecture degree.

Pei received the Medal of Liberty from President Ronald Reagan in 1986. In 1993, he was awarded the Presidential Medal of Freedom, the highest civilian honor in the United States, in recognition of his cultural contributions to his adopted country. He has also received awards from France and Japan honoring his achievements.

Music

Music and musicians have always been highly regarded in China. Music is viewed as a way for people to connect to the natural world. As far back as 3,400 years, sophisticated musical instruments were part of Chinese culture. During the Han Dynasty (206 B.C.–A.D. 220), a Music Bureau was established to collect ancient folk music.

Chinese instrumentalists and singers try to make their music as expressive as poetry. The "color" or intonation of each note is emphasized, rather than a specific melody. The goal of the performance is to achieve harmony with the surroundings.

Chinese music is based on a five-tone scale. Traditional stringed instruments include zithers such as the *qin* and *zheng*, a lute-like instrument called a *pipa*, and the *erhu*, a two-stringed fiddle. Musicians pluck the strings of the *pipa* with their long fingernails. Bamboo flutes such as the *xiao* and *di* are also traditional instruments. They are usually featured in Chinese opera, along with the *pipa* and the *erhu*.

While traditional Chinese folk music is kept alive in many communities, Chinese Americans enjoy many other types of music as well, including symphony orchestras, rock groups, and other Western musical forms.

Spotlight on
YO-YO MA

Yo-Yo Ma, winner of ten Grammy awards, began playing the cello at age four. His father was his first teacher. Ma played a Bach cello suite in his first recital at age six. When Ma and his family moved to the United States, his playing came to the attention of several prominent musicians, including violinist Isaac Stern, who recommended Ma to instructors at the Juilliard School for the Performing Arts in New York City.

In 1964, Yo-Yo Ma made his American debut at Carnegie Hall in New York. He was nine years old. He continued to study at Juilliard until he was sixteen and then went to Harvard. In 1978, Ma was awarded the Avery Fisher Prize for his outstanding achievement and excellence in music. This honor allowed him to perform with the leading orchestras around the country.

Ma continues to record music and to perform as well as teaching promising young musicians.

• • • • • •

Theater and Chinese opera were a part of Chinese life until the mid-1950s. In the twentieth century, as the movie industry grew, its popularity exploded in China. From early martial arts movies to today's sophisticated art films, Chinese filmmakers have influenced the growth of movies. Today, many Chinese and Chinese American actors and directors are respected names in the U.S. film industry.

Food

Food is an important part of the Chinese culture. No gathering of family or friends is complete without it. Festivals and holidays are often celebrated with a feast, demonstrating the wealth and generosity of the host family.

In Chinese tradition, cooking is considered an art and has been influenced by both Confucian and Taoist philosophies. Confucianism stresses that the flavors of the ingredients must blend until there is harmony. The appearance of a dish is also important; color and texture are as important as taste. Taoism, with its emphasis on living a long life, developed sanitary cooking practices. It also identified foods that would lead to a longer life.

Cutting foods into small pieces before cooking is fundamental to Chinese cooking. This practice came about because fuel was scarce in many parts of China. Cutting the food into small pieces allows it to cook quickly over a small hot fire. This process is called stir-frying and is very popular in America today. This practice also enables diners to eat without many utensils.

Since China is such a large country, it is not surprising that cooking styles and specialties vary from one region to another. Cantonese

The Fortune Cookie

Although no one knows for sure how fortune cookies came to be, one thing is certain—they're not Chinese. Some give credit for the invention of the fortune cookie to David Jung of the Hong Kong Noodle Factory in Los Angeles. The story is that he invented the cookie in 1918 to provide hope for the many unemployed workers who gathered near Jung's restaurant. Of course, if the fortune cookies motivated people to eat at Jung's noodle house, that was good too. Today, American fortune cookie factories export the sweet treats to China and Hong Kong, as well as selling them throughout the United States.

dishes often feature roasted or grilled meats. Fried rice, chow mein, and shark's fin soup are well-known Cantonese dishes. The eastern province of Fukien is known for many types of soups and seafood dishes, while the Peking-Shantung region excels in the use of spices and seasonings. Sweet-and-sour dishes come from the Honan province in central China, while Szechuan-Hunan cooking offers hot, spicy food.

Americans have embraced Chinese cooking with enthusiasm. Today, many Chinese dishes have become as much a part of American culture as pizza and tacos.

Food as Medicine

For many Chinese, there is little difference between food and medicine. Over the centuries, medicinal values for thousands of plants, roots, seeds, fungi, and herbs have been recorded. For instance, ginger relieves an upset stomach, and ginseng strengthens the heart. Chinese herbalists are graduates of a Chinese traditional medical school. As such, they are given the same privileges in China as doctors in Western countries.

Tea

Tea drinking has been part of Chinese culture for over a thousand years. It developed into an art form during the Tang Dynasty, when Lu Yu, the Father of Tea, wrote a book called *Tea Classic*. The book described the planting and growing of tea, its preparation, and a tea ceremony requiring twenty-seven pieces of equipment that would have been conducted by wealthy or noble Chinese. A special tea ceremony is conducted at traditional Chinese weddings. But most tea ceremonies are performed for the enjoyment of friends: no special occasion is necessary. These ceremonies focus on the sensory experience of smelling and tasting different teas.

As tea production was refined over the years, three different types of tea—green, oolong, and black—were developed. Their differences are based on the amount of fermentation, or drying, that takes place in the tea leaves. Teas are sometimes scented with flowers, such as jasmine, for added aroma.

Today, more tea is consumed worldwide than any other drink besides water. Medical research is beginning to support claims that tea has medicinal qualities. Some studies have shown that tea can lower cholesterol, protect against heart disease and stroke, and fight cancer-causing agents.

Tea Facts

• Over 90 percent of the world's tea comes from Asian countries.

• Tea plants must grow for at least five years before leaves can be picked.

• When a tea plant reaches thirty years of age, it is no longer productive. The trunk is cut off and new stems grow from the roots. The roots of a tea plant may grow for a hundred years.

• Tea leaves are picked by hand. An experienced picker gathers about a pound of green leaves each day.

• Each tea tree will be harvested twenty to thirty times during the picking season, about once a week.

• It generally takes 4 pounds (1.8 kilograms) of fresh leaves to produce 1 pound (0.45 kilogram) of dry tea. One of the highest quality Chinese teas, Dragon Well, is gathered when the leaves are just beginning to grow. It takes about 60,000 leaves to make 2 pounds (0.9 kilogram) of this prized green tea. In the past, Dragon Well tea was served only to the emperor's household.

Source: China, The Homeland of Tea
(www.AsiaRecipe.com/chitea.html)

Tomato Beef

8 ounces flank steak, well trimmed

1/4 teaspoon baking soda

1-1/2 teaspoons soy sauce

1-1/2 teaspoons cornstarch

1 teaspoon Shao Hsing rice cooking wine

1/4 teaspoon sesame oil

1-1/4 teaspoons sugar

5 tomatoes, about 2 pounds

1 teaspoon plus 1 tablespoon vegetable oil

6 slices ginger

3 tablespoons oyster sauce

4 scallions, cut into 2-inch sections

Halve the flank steak with the grain into 2 strips. Cut each strip across the grain into 1/4-inch-thick slices. Place slices in a shallow bowl and sprinkle with the baking soda. Stir to combine. Add the soy sauce, cornstarch, rice wine, sesame oil, and 1/4 teaspoon sugar. Stir to combine and set aside.

In a large pot, bring about 1-1/2 quarts of water to a boil. Add the tomatoes and cook 1 to 3 minutes, or until the tomato skins just break. Remove tomatoes with a slotted spoon. When they are cool enough to handle, peel the skins off. Core the tomatoes and cut into 1/2-inch-thick wedges.

Meanwhile, stir 1 teaspoon vegetable oil into the beef mixture. Heat a 14-inch flat-bottomed wok or skillet over high heat until hot but not smoking. Add the remaining tablespoon vegetable oil and the ginger. Stir-fry about 1 minute. Carefully add the beef, spreading it in the wok. Cook, undisturbed, 1 to 2 minutes, letting beef begin to brown. Then, using a metal spatula, stir-fry 1 to 2 minutes, or until beef is browned but still slightly rare. Transfer the beef to a plate and set aside.

Add the tomatoes and remaining teaspoon of sugar to wok. Stir-fry 1 minute on high heat until tomatoes begin to soften. Add the oyster sauce and 1/4 cup cold water. Cover and cook 2 to 3 minutes, or until the tomatoes are just limp. Add scallions and the beef, along with any juices that have accumulated on the plate. Stir-fry 1 minute, or until just heated through. Serve immediately.

Serves 4 to 6 as part of a multi-course meal.

Source: Adapted from The Wisdom of the Chinese Kitchen *by Grace Young*

CHAPTER FOUR

Colombians

Colombia,

situated at the northern tip of South America, is the gateway between North and South America. It is a large country, about the size of Texas and California combined. Constant violence and crime have forced hundreds of thousands of Colombians to seek political *asylum,* or safety, in the United States.

A Quick Look Back

Although several native tribes were well established in the region, Colombia's written history didn't begin until the Spanish began settling the area in the early 1500s. By the early 1700s, the Spanish had conquered what are now Colombia, Venezuela, Ecuador, and Panama. They called the region New Granada. As the Spanish settlers arrived, they took the best land for their farms. The native people were treated as slaves, forced to work on the farms and in emerald mines. When the native population dwindled due to overwork and diseases brought by the colonists, slaves were brought in from Africa.

Many people in New Granada grew increasingly frustrated with the Spanish rule. There was no opportunity for advancement economically, socially, or politically unless one was born in Spain. Encouraged by the successful revolutions in America and France, they rebelled.

Led by Simón Bolívar, the nationalists overcame the Spanish government in 1819. They established the *Gran Colombia* (Greater Colombia) *republic.* It initially included the territories of Colombia and Panama. Venezuela and Ecuador joined the republic when they won their independence from Spain in 1821 and 1822, respectively. Eight years later, Venezuela, Ecuador, and Panama withdrew from the republic and became independent nations.

The Republic of Colombia

Free from Spain's rule, Colombia established a republic. Its constitution called for a president to be elected from one of the two traditional parties, the Liberals and the Conservatives. The Liberals were in favor of a *decentralized government,* in which the power is shared by state and federal offices. They also wanted separation of church and state, a school system that was independent of the Roman Catholic Church, voting rights for everyone, and an end to slavery.

The Roman Catholic Church was a very powerful entity in Colombia. It controlled large tracts of land and had a strong influence on the Conservative Party. The Conservatives wanted to establish a central government that maintained its close connection with the Roman Catholic Church. In this form of government, decisions are made by the president and legislature and handed down to the departments, or states, to carry out. One of the decisions was that Catholicism was the only religion that could be practiced.

Power moved between the two groups for over 100 years, marked at times by fighting and civil war. Nothing, however, prepared the people for the violence that was to come.

Visitors admire the statue of Simón Bolívar in Washington, D.C. The statue, 27 feet (8 meters) tall, is the tallest statue in Washington and reported to be the largest equestrian statue in the United States.

Fast Facts

- Miami is closer to Colombia's Caribbean coast than to New York.

- The southeastern part of Colombia is part of the Amazon rain forest.

- Colombia is one of the top five suppliers of oil to the United States.

- Nearly four-fifths of all carnations and one-third of all roses sold in the United States are grown in Colombia.

- Colombia produces more emeralds than any other country in the world.

Source: Embassy of Colombia (www.colombiaemb.org)

La Violencia

In the 1930s and 1940s, Jorge Gaitán was a popular Liberal political leader. He fought for better conditions for the poor and working class in Colombia. In 1948, Gaitán was assassinated in Bogotá. People lashed out in anger and frustration, kicking off the worst civil war in Colombia's history. Violent fighting took place in the rural areas as well as in the cities. By the time the fighting settled down, nearly ten years later, over 300,000 were dead and much of the country was destroyed. Known as La Violencia, this decade of violence triggered a mass migration from the countryside to the cities. It also created an environment that helped establish the *guerrilla* (ge-RILL-a) movement. Guerrillas are similar to soldiers, but they usually fight against the government. They work in small groups so they can strike quickly and then escape.

opposite page: Manuel Marulanda (second from right), the founder and commander of the Revolutionary Armed Forces of Colombia (FARC), stands with other revolutionary leaders and soldiers in the FARC-controlled zone of Colombia. The FARC is the oldest and largest rebel group in Colombia. It numbers over 15,000.

The National Front

Laureano Gómez Castro was the Conservative president during the early La Violencia period. He began ruling as a *dictator,* rather than a president, and was removed from office by a military group. The country remained under military control until 1957. Liberal and Conservative leaders decided that they had to work together to end the violence and get the country moving forward again. They formed the National Front, a coalition party in which Liberals and Conservatives shared power, switching presidents every four years.

Although some progress was made, the economy remained depressed. People had trouble finding jobs. Finally,

The Colombian Guerrilla Movement

During the decade of La Violencia, groups of peasants began to arm themselves. These small groups grew to become the guerrilla movement. They fought mostly in the countryside, attacking the wealthy, the corporations, and the government. Later, some of the groups demanded money from drug farmers and traffickers to protect their operations. Peace talks have been held with varying success over the past twenty years. In early 2002, the latest peace process disintegrated into war once again.

in the late 1960s, President Carlos Lleras Restrepo introduced reforms that improved conditions for many Colombians. He also helped introduce political changes that ended the National Front. In 1974, normal elections were held for the first time in twenty-five years.

Drug Wars

High unemployment and increasing uneasiness marked the end of the 1970s in Colombia. The guerrillas were still fighting in the countryside, and the army was having trouble controlling them. By the early 1980s, the guerrilla attacks had escalated. Kidnappings, murders, and political assassinations seemed like everyday occurrences. An amnesty program was initiated in the early 1980s in which about 400 guerrillas took part. A truce was announced between the government and the rebels in 1984, but it didn't last long.

At this same time, groups called *cartels* began producing cocaine and smuggling it into the United States and Europe. As the government tried to end the drug trafficking, some of the guerrillas and the cartels agreed to work together. Financed with drug money, the heavily armed guerrillas provided protection for the drug traffickers. The increasing strength of the guerrillas made it hard for the Colombian army to control either the drug cartels or the guerrillas. The guerrillas continued terrorizing the country with bombings and kidnappings for ransom, while the flow of drugs into the United States and Europe escalated.

Wealthy landowners in rural areas began forming private armies, called paramilitary groups, for protection from the guerrillas. Evidence shows that some of the paramilitary groups are linked to the Colombian army. The poor people living in rural areas were caught between the paramilitary groups and the guerrillas. In many cases, a paramilitary group took over a village, killing anyone suspected of supporting the guerrillas. When the group left, the guerrillas would return and kill anyone suspected of supporting the paramilitaries. As the violence grew, thousands of poor Colombians fled to the cities. Those who could afford to leave the country sought political asylum in other countries, including the United States.

With increasing power, the cartels grew even more dangerous, and the government increased its arrests of suspected drug traffickers. The cartels responded by assassinating three presidential candidates. During the 1990s, the government successfully destroyed the two main cartels, the Medellin and the Cali, but not before thousands of Colombians had lost their lives. Smaller, more mobile groups of drug traffickers quickly replaced the cartels. Drug trafficking continues today.

Colombia Today

Peace talks between the paramilitary groups, the guerrillas, and the government were held from 1999 to 2002, but they failed to accomplish anything. Colombia's newest president, Alvaro Uribe, won the election by promising to get tough on both the paramilitary groups and the guerrillas. Uribe was supported by many of the Colombians who are living in exile in the United States. His pledge to fight the guerrillas and the paramilitary groups that terrorize the country leads the exiles to hope that they may be able to return home someday.

Rebel soldiers of the Maoist People's Liberation Army (EPL) patrol the streets of La Gabarra, about 290 miles (464 kilometers) northeast of Bogotá.

Colombian Population in the U.S.	
Florida	190,445
New York	111,267
New Jersey	89,866
California	32,076
Source: U.S. Census, 2000	

Coming to America

W hen a *civil war* pitting guerrilla forces against the government broke out in the 1950s, people began leaving Colombia. The numbers increased dramatically when drug production and trafficking became widespread in the 1980s. Increased threats of kidnapping combined with high unemployment have encouraged an estimated 1.1 million people to leave Colombia since 1996. Of those who stay, over 3,500 are killed each year as a result of the fighting in Colombia.

Today, over half a million Colombians live in the United States, primarily in Florida and New York. Many consider themselves to be exiles, waiting for peace to return to their country so they

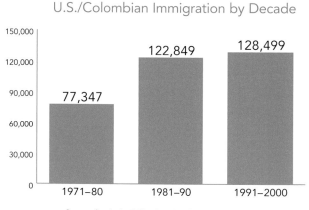

U.S./Colombian Immigration by Decade

Source: Statistical Yearbook of the Immigration and Naturalization Service

can return home. Others have become American citizens and are actively involved in politics and community affairs in the United States.

Life in America

Colombians have settled in nearly every state in America, although the largest communities are found in Miami, Florida, and New York City, areas where Spanish language and culture have been established for years. Coming from a country that shares many characteristics with the United States, including a diverse ethnic population, a democratic government, and freedom of religion, many of the exiles have found it relatively easy to adapt to life in America. Things are tougher for those who aren't fluent in English or who have had to leave their families behind.

Family

In the United States, Colombian families work hard to preserve the closeness that is so important to their way of life. Colombians are used to living with their extended families, supporting each other, taking care of elderly relatives or young children. The recent violence and kidnappings have split many families as those threatened with death have fled the country, leaving spouses and children behind. Once they arrive in America, many Colombians will form surrogate families out of friends and acquaintances. The sense of belonging to a group becomes even more important to them as they struggle to make new lives for themselves.

Work

The Colombians who have come to the United States are, for the most part, professionals from the middle and upper classes. The strong work ethic that is valued in the Colombian culture is helping them find success in America as well, although most initially have to accept blue-collar jobs due to their lack of fluency in English.

As Colombians have settled in the United States, many have become citizens. They are now beginning to run for local, state, and federal offices in order to make their voices heard.

Spotlight on
JUAN PABLO MONTOYA

Juan Pablo Montoya celebrates his victory in the Indianapolis 500 in May 2000.

Born in Bogotá, Colombia, Juan Pablo Montoya is considered by some racing fans to be the most promising race-car driver today. He began his formula 1 racing career in 1997. In 1999, at the age of 24, Montoya won the Championship Auto Racing Teams (CART) championship series, making him the youngest champion in the history of the series. The next year Montoya became the first person to win the Indianapolis 500 in his first attempt.

Although his 2001 season was plagued with mechanical difficulties, Montoya finished the 2002 formula 1 series season in third place.

School

Children arriving in the United States from Colombia have an easier time than many other *immigrant* groups. The popular culture of America is similar to that in Colombia's bigger cities. Music, movies, and media are accessible to students, so they feel "in step" with American kids as soon as they arrive. The emphasis on education in Colombia also prepares children for the academic goals set by most American schools, although the wealthier immigrant whose family sent them to private school in Colombia does have an easier time. The language barrier is the greatest obstacle facing Colombian students who immigrate to America, but the international nature of their home country has often given them a basic knowledge of English. Even without that knowledge, because Spanish is a language commonly heard throughout the United States, Colombian students are still able to adapt more quickly than immigrants from other countries.

Religion

The Spanish introduced Roman Catholicism to the region when it conquered Colombia and its neighbors. The Roman Catholic Church played a significant role in the history of Colombia. Today, nearly everyone (95 percent) is Catholic.

Roman Catholicism

Christianity is made up of many different groups. All of these groups believe that Jesus Christ is the son of God. Although they share many beliefs, each group has a different understanding of the Bible and Jesus' teachings.

As Christianity spread, churches were named after the cities where they were built. All of these churches together were called the catholic church. In this case, catholic means one universal church. The church that was built in Rome became known as the Roman Catholic Church. That name is used today to refer to the specific religious group.

The pope is the leader of the Roman Catholic Church. Roman Catholics believe that the pope has the final word in church policy.

Other major beliefs of the Roman Catholic Church are:

• Through sacraments (religious ceremonies) such as Baptism and Holy Communion, God grants people the grace and strength to live holy lives.

• Followers of Catholicism can be saved from their sins or wrongdoing through faith and good works.

Holidays and Festivals

Colombians celebrate many of the same holidays as Americans, including New Year's Day, Easter, All Saint's Day, and Christmas. The Christmas celebration, called Las Novenas (lahs noh-BAY-nahs), begins nine days before Christmas. These days are full of parties and religious customs. On Christmas Eve, families gather to enjoy a large dinner, sing carols, and exchange gifts. Children wake up on Christmas morning anxious to find their gifts from the baby Jesus.

Colombian Americans, especially those who live in Florida and New York, continue to celebrate Colombian Independence Day (July 20). At this time, associations of Colombian Americans, such as the Colombian American Service Association in Miami, sponsor events that help immigrants preserve and celebrate their heritage.

The Arts

Music and dance are very important in the Colombian culture. Colombia's most famous musical forms—*vallenato* and *cumbia*—are rooted in the heritage of the native people and the slaves who were brought from West Africa.

Vallenato, Colombian accordion music, began in the northeastern region of Colombia but quickly gained popularity across the country. *Vallenato* mixes accordions, bass, and percussion into energetic dance music. It draws much of its style from the music of the native peoples. The underlying rhythm shows the influence of music from Africa as well. The songs' lyrics are always about love and life in the villages of rural Colombia.

Cumbia music began along the coast of Colombia. It mixes African rhythms with elements of Cuban music. Until recently, *cumbia* was considered music for the lower classes, given its association with black communities. Today it is considered the national sound of Colombia. Its rhythms are heard in many types of music, from mambo to hip-hop.

Colombian Americans keep their traditional dances alive through groups such as El Grupo Esmeralda in Miami, Florida. The high school and college students that make up this group perform Colombian folkloric dances at special events around the city.

Café de Colombia

What would you do if you noticed some goats jumping around with lots of energy? According to legend, this is how coffee was discovered! An Ethiopian goatherder named Kaldi noticed that his goats had more energy after eating the leaves and berries of a coffee shrub. He tried making a drink from the berries and found that he, too, felt refreshed. Word spread of the new drink, and before long, coffee became a precious trading commodity.

Arabs were the first people to grow coffee commercially. Recognizing the value of coffee beans, they guarded the trees like gold. It wasn't until a tree was stolen and smuggled out of the country that production began elsewhere. In the 1600s, coffee arrived in Europe, where it became known as Arabian wine.

By 1835, coffee trees were being grown commercially in Colombia. More and more trees were planted as the seeds were carried throughout the country on foot and by train. One story explains that the coffee trees spread rapidly when a priest assigned the planting of trees as a penance for sin.

Farming coffee is difficult work. First, workers must pick the coffee berries by hand when they are bright red. The ripe berries are put in bags to be taken to a machine that removes the pulp (the fleshy red part). The beans that remain are what will eventually become coffee.

The beans are soaked for twenty-four hours and then carefully washed. Workers spread the beans in bright sunny areas and stir them until they are dry. Each night, the beans are covered to protect them from moisture. After inspectors check the quality of the beans, they are placed in a machine that takes off the husk. The beans are now ready to be roasted. As they are roasted, the coffee beans double in size.

Food

In Colombia, the main meal of the day is usually eaten at lunch. Many businesses close from noon until 2 p.m., allowing families to eat their meal together. Colombians living in the United States generally have their main meal in the evening, as lunch is often a rushed event. Most ingredients for traditional Colombian dishes can easily be found in the United States, so immigrants can enjoy a taste of home whenever they wish.

Colombia has rich, fertile land that provides a variety of foods. Corn, potatoes, chicken, beans, and rice are all staples of the Colombian diet. The capital city of Bogotá is known for its thick chicken and potato soup, Ajiaco Bogotano (ah-hee-AH-koh boh-goh-TAH-no). *Arepas,* corn cakes cooked on a griddle, are popular throughout Colombia.

Recipe

Ajiaco Bogotano

1 3-1/2- to 4-pound chicken, cut into pieces

8 cups chicken stock

1 large onion, cut in half

1 bay leaf

1/2 teaspoon cumin seeds, ground

1/4 teaspoon thyme

Salt and pepper to taste

2 pounds assorted potatoes, peeled and coarsely chopped

3 ears of corn, cut into 2-inch slices

1 cup heavy cream at room temperature

2 tablespoons capers, rinsed and drained

1 avocado, thinly sliced

Combine the chicken and the stock. Bring to a boil. Add the onion, bay leaf, cumin, thyme, and salt and pepper. Reduce the heat and simmer, uncovered, for 30 minutes or until the chicken is very tender.

Remove the chicken from the stock and take the meat from the bones. Cut the meat into thin strips and discard the skin and bones.

Strain the stock and return it to the pot. Bring it to a boil and add the potatoes. Cook them until they are very soft and can be mashed against the side of the pot. Add the corn and the chicken meat. Simmer, uncovered, just until the corn is cooked, about 5 minutes.

To serve, divide the cream and the capers among 6 generous soup plates. Add the soup, garnish with thin slices of avocado, and serve immediately. Or place the chicken meat, corn, sliced avocado, cream, and capers into separate serving bowls. Ladle the soup into 6 generous soup plates and let the diners add what they like to the basic soup.

Serves 6.

Source: Adapted from South American Cooking *by Barbara Karoff*

CHAPTER FIVE

Cubans

Cuba,

a small island nation located only 90 miles (145 kilometers) south of Florida, has had an often uneasy relationship with the United States. Colonized by the Spanish government in the early 1500s, Cuba won its independence from Spain in 1898 following the Spanish-American War. But the United States, concerned with protecting the interests of U.S. citizens who owned businesses or land in Cuba, demanded that Cuba give the United States the right to approve treaties and make other governmental decisions.

Economic problems and government corruption led to periods of unrest. Cubans banded together to demand reforms. Mostly, they wanted control of their own destiny with no intervention from the United States. In 1940, Cuba adopted a new constitution. During the late 1940s and early 1950s, corruption in the government increased greatly. Higher prices created hardships for the many poor people in Cuba. A former president, Fulgencio Batista (ba-TEEST-ta), took control of the government by force and established a dictatorship.

Many groups opposed Batista, but the revolutionary army led by Fidel Castro received most of the support. After two years of fighting, Castro's troops gained control of Cuba in 1959. People welcomed the change in leadership, believing that Castro would recognize the 1940 constitution and hold democratic elections once more. Within months, however, many people realized that the communist-minded Castro did not intend to lead a democracy. Those who opposed his socialist plans fled to safety in the United States. They began an exodus that continues today.

A Quick Look Back

Struggles for independence have marked Cuba's history. After the conquest by Spain in the early 1500s, the native people of Cuba suffered the same fate as those in other Caribbean and Latin American countries. They were forced to work for the colonists until malnutrition, disease, and overwork destroyed their population. The Spanish then brought in slaves from West Africa to work in the sugarcane fields. The slaves in Cuba were allowed to purchase their freedom. By 1774, there was a sizable population of free blacks and mulattoes (people with both Spanish and black ancestry).

As the nineteenth century began, many Cubans wanted changes in their government. Some supported offers by the United States to purchase Cuba from Spain and make it an American territory. Others wanted to remain under Spain's protection, but with more control over their local government. A third group wanted complete independence from both Spain and the United States.

The Independence Movement

The Ten Years' War began in 1868 as a demand for reforms in taxes, representation, and racial equality. When Spain refused to agree to changes, a sugar planter named Carlos Manuel de Céspedes led the fight for freedom from Spanish rule. Many blacks and mulattoes joined the *guerrillas* in the fight for independence. But after ten long years of fighting, most of the rebels accepted amnesty in return for an end to the war. Some left for the United States and other countries, where they planned new strategies for gaining Cuba's independence.

In the late 1800s, José Martí formed the Cuban Revolutionary Party to unite several different rebel groups. By 1895, the independence movement had gained control of most of Cuba. Spain fought back with actions that killed an estimated 20 percent of the Cuban population. When an American ship exploded in the Havana harbor, the United States entered the conflict.

The Spanish-American War, fought in 1898, ended quickly. Spain turned over control of Cuba to the United States. Although the Cuban independence groups had been fighting for thirty years for freedom, the United States soon had complete control of the island.

The Platt Amendment

At the end of the Spanish-American War, Cuba was declared independent of Spain, but the United States was given complete control of the country. Cubans were excluded from the negotiations, which caused resentment among them. During the three and a half years that the United States occupied Cuba, the government built schools, bridges, roads, and sanitation systems and established programs to kill the mosquitoes that carried malaria.

At that time, many Americans felt strongly that Cuba rightfully belonged to the United States. They were determined to set up an Americanized system of government. Cubans were allowed to elect their leaders, but the United States insisted that conditions protecting American interests should be added to the constitution. The resulting conditions, called the Platt Amendment, gave the United States control over a supposedly independent Cuba. It included the following provisions:

- Cuba couldn't make treaties with other countries.
- Cuba had to sell or lease land to the United States for use as military bases.
- Restrictions were placed on foreign loans.
- Cuba had to establish specific health care measures.
- The United States could approve presidential candidates.
- The United States could intervene if conditions in Cuba were unstable.

Although Cubans detested the Platt Amendment, the United States would not end its military occupation until the amendment had been added to the constitution. So, in 1901, the Platt Amendment finally became part of the Cuban constitution. The United States withdrew from Cuba in 1902.

Early 1900s

From 1902 until 1934, the Platt Amendment allowed the United States to send troops to Cuba whenever economic instability or political unrest caused problems there. With an economy based on one product—sugar—Cuba was vulnerable to changes in the market. The United States military was forced to intervene in 1908 and in 1912 when instability threatened. When the market fell in 1920, the poor and working class struggled for survival. Many groups began to call for social justice and equality.

In 1924, Gerardo Machado was elected president. He implemented programs that were very popular and promised to amend the Platt Amendment. Beginning in 1928, however, economic problems destroyed the remaining years of his presidency. When the Great Depression hit and the price of sugar dropped, Machado's popularity fell as well. People gathered in protest, demanding jobs and unions. Machado outlawed these demonstrations. He set up a secret police force to round up and execute anyone who spoke out against his government. Machado was finally forced out of office in 1933.

The appointment of Carlos Manuel de Céspedes as interim president by the United States infuriated Cubans. A sergeant in the army, Fulgencio Batista, took control of the military. Within weeks, Batista forced Céspedes to resign

Colonel Fulgencio Batista (center before the microphone) takes the oath of office as president of Cuba in Havana in 1940.

office. The Cubans made Ramón Grau San Martín, a professor at Havana's law school, the new president. Grau focused on government reforms, such as abolishing the Platt Amendment, redistributing land ownership, and creating a fair taxation system. Cuban conservatives thought that Grau's reforms would take away their wealth, while the Communists urged Grau to make more drastic changes. Without support from either side, Grau was easily forced from office in 1934.

Batista led the *coup,* but he didn't take Grau's place as president. Instead he allowed others to serve as president while he built a strong power base. Then, in 1940, Batista was elected president. Under his leadership, many rebel leaders were arrested and executed. However, his programs were supported by the middle-class and wealthy Cubans who benefited from the peace and stability that resulted. Batista served as president until 1944, then left Cuba to live in the United States.

Revolution

The next eight years were highlighted by two of the most corrupt governments that Cuba ever had. At the same time, prices for everyday goods and services rose dramatically. Poor people were struggling to make enough to survive, while the wealthy made more money than ever before. Conditions were ripe for change.

In the early 1950s, as cries for political reform were raised, Fulgencio Batista returned to Cuba to run for office. When he realized he wasn't going to win the election, Batista took control of the government and declared himself a *dictator.* Outraged, the Cuban people formed opposition groups to fight against his government.

A young lawyer named Fidel Castro was the leader of one of these opposition groups. He and his followers attempted to overthrow Batista twice before they were successful. Their daring guerrilla attacks against Batista's superior forces made the revolutionaries heroes in the eyes of many Cubans. Support for Castro grew. Batista, realizing that he would soon be removed from office, secretly boarded a plane on December 31, 1958, and left Cuba.

Castro Gains Power

When Fidel Castro's rebels gained control of the government in January 1959, he promised that elections would be held within one year and that the constitution would be followed again. He championed a program that taught Cubans to read and write. Hospitals were built in rural areas. Castro denied at first that he was a Communist, but it soon became apparent that he had lied. Although the urban working classes and farm workers (who were the majority of people in Cuba) welcomed these changes, the middle and upper classes suspected that Castro would not return the government to democracy. They began to leave Cuba.

The United States government watched Castro's movements very carefully. Economic sanctions were used to pressure Castro to maintain a democratic government. A blockade of Cuba's major ports stopped shipments of oil, food, and other goods that Cubans depended upon. Castro ignored the sanctions and continued to authorize government takeovers of businesses and plantations, many of them owned by U.S. citizens. At the same time, Castro turned to the Soviet Union for economic assistance.

The prospect of a Communist country as a neighbor was frightening to the U.S. government. Cuba's location close to the United States would make it easy to launch an attack on America. When it became apparent that Castro was establishing a Communist government, the Central Intelligence Agency began training Cuban exiles to invade Cuba. Their goal was to overthrow Castro's government.

Fidel Castro is shown with some of his supporters at his guerrilla headquarters in the Cuban mountains in 1957.

The operation, known today as the Bay of Pigs invasion, was a disaster. Several hundred exiles were killed, and over a thousand were imprisoned. Soon after Castro's victory, he formed an alliance with the Soviet Union, which provided economic aid as well as military weapons and training.

The Cuban Missile Crisis

When Nikita Khrushchev (nee-kee-tah kruush-CHAWF) replaced Joseph Stalin as the leader of the Soviet Union, he appeared to be open to talks about limiting nuclear arms. Some of the tension of the Cold War relaxed. Then, in October 1962, U.S. military planes flying over Cuba photographed Soviet nuclear missiles on the island. From these bases, nuclear attacks could be launched against any major U.S. city.

President John Kennedy faced a dangerous, delicate situation. The wrong move could set off nuclear war, destroying both the United States and the Soviet Union. Kennedy and his advisers agreed to send U.S. battleships to close off the Havana harbor. The Soviets were warned that any attempt to enter the harbor would result in a nuclear attack on their country. The quarantine allowed the countries to try to resolve the situation peacefully before starting actions that would almost certainly kill millions of people.

Khrushchev, having underestimated the United States' determination to defend itself, was forced to withdraw the missiles. At the last minute, the potential catastrophe was prevented. This close brush with nuclear war brought a new resolve from both countries to negotiate arms control.

Cuba Today

opposite page:
This Department of Defense photo shows Soviet missile equipment being loaded at the Mariel naval port in 1962. Photos such as this proved that the Soviets had placed strategic missiles in Cuba.

Fidel Castro continues to rule Cuba, more than forty years after he first gained power. Economic sanctions are still in place, but they have had little effect on the Communist Party leaders. With their special privileges, they can still afford to purchase items on the black market. The poor people, who have little control over their government's decisions, are the ones who suffer the effects of the embargo. While debate continues about whether the economic sanctions imposed by the United States should be lifted or kept in place, Cuban refugees still make their way to America.

TRAILERS

2 MISSILE TRANSPORTERS

OXIDIZER TRAILER

6 MISSILE TRANSPORTERS

ROB IRBM
LANT TRAILERS

ERECTOR

The Cold War

The Cold War began within months after World War II ended. The Soviet Union, with its Communist government, was intent on expanding its power into Eastern Europe. The United States and its allies were just as determined to stop the spread of *Communism*. The Soviet Union and the United States didn't fight each other directly during the Cold War. Instead, they supported opposite sides in Third World countries whose political unrest had erupted into *civil war*.

During the Cold War, both the Soviet Union and the United States rushed to build powerful weapons, including nuclear missiles. People everywhere feared that a nuclear war between the two superpowers was unavoidable. Some Americans built fallout shelters in their backyards. Schools held nuclear safety drills in addition to fire drills. In the midst of these fears, Nikita Khrushchev, the leader of the Soviet Union, agreed to support Fidel Castro's government in Cuba. America's worst enemy was on friendly terms with one of our closest neighbors.

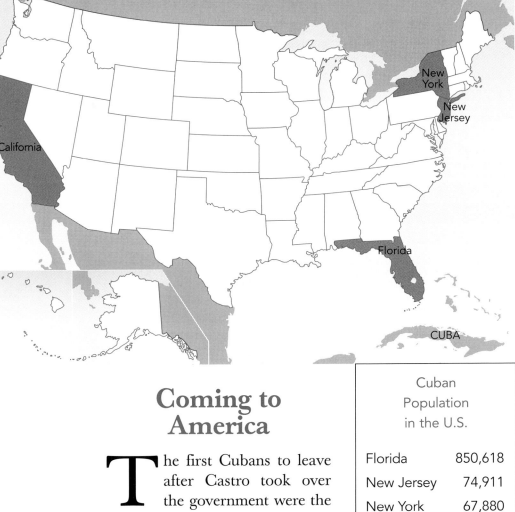

Coming to America

Cuban Population in the U.S.	
Florida	850,618
New Jersey	74,911
New York	67,880
California	64,191

Source: U.S. Census, 2000

T he first Cubans to leave after Castro took over the government were the Batista supporters. Facing torture and death, they fled to nearby countries, including the United States. Within months, they were followed by the wealthy land and business owners who protested Castro's new policies limiting land ownership, seizing and nationalizing businesses, and ending the free press, among others. From early 1961 to 1962, the educated, professional, middle class began leaving Cuba. Most went to Miami, Florida. A Cuban *Refugee* Center was established there to help the new arrivals adjust to life in America.

U.S./Cuban Immigration by Decade

Decade	Immigrants
1971–80	264,863
1981–90	144,578
1991–2000	169,322

Source: Statistical Yearbook of the Immigration and Naturalization Service

Recognizing that most of the opposition to his *regime* would come from this group of wealthy and educated professionals, Castro encouraged them to leave the country. After they left, he seized their property and announced that they were traitors. The *exiles* could never return home as long as Castro was in power.

Most of the early Cuban exiles believed that Castro would be over-thrown within a short time. It was always in their plans to return when Castro was no longer in charge. For the earliest exiles, those few years have stretched into decades. Most have settled into their lives in America, but they continue to take an avid interest in the island of their birth.

> **"Next year in Cuba!"**
> This declaration, commonly heard at Christmas, reminds Cuban Americans of the exiled community that longed to return home.

Operation Pedro Pan

During this period, Cuban parents faced a heart-wrenching decision: keep their children with them in Cuba or send them to safety in America. People were afraid that Castro would take their children away and brainwash them into becoming *Communists,* perhaps even send them to the Soviet Union. Young boys would have to serve in Castro's military. The Catholic Church in Miami sponsored a program called Operation Pedro Pan, named after the fictional leader of the Lost Boys in the book *Peter Pan.* (*Pedro* is Spanish for "Peter.") The program allowed children ages six to sixteen to stay in southern Florida until their parents could reach America or until the children were adopted by American families. Over 14,000 children left Cuba between 1961 and 1963 as part of this program. Many never saw their parents again.

Freedom Flights

After the Cuban missile crisis in 1962 in which the United States forced the Soviet Union to withdraw nuclear missiles they had situated in Cuba, Cubans had a more diffi-cult time leaving their island. There were no flights to the United States, so they had to travel by sea. Small boats, rafts, even inner tubes were used by people desperate to reach America. For the first time, people from the working class were among those leaving Cuba.

In 1965, Castro made a surprise announcement—Cuban exiles could return to the port of Camarioca, Cuba, to pick up any relatives who wished to leave Cuba. There were some restrictions, though. No professional or skilled workers were allowed to leave. Men between fifteen and twenty-six had to remain in Cuba and serve in the military. The Cuban government would take over the homes and property of those who left.

Despite these restrictions, Camarioca was soon crowded with working-class Cubans who wanted to leave, as well as Cuban exiles who were trying to find family members. The American government negotiated with Castro to allow people to leave by plane after their visas were processed. The "Freedom Flights" flew twice a day, five days a week, from December 1965 until 1971, when President Richard Nixon ended the program. Over 250,000 Cubans took advantage of the program.

In 1966, Congress passed a law giving *asylum* to all Cubans who came to the United States. As refugees, they became eligible for government programs, including public assistance, English classes, scholarships, and student loans.

The Mariel Boatlift

The 1970s brought increasing discontent to Cuba. There were severe food shortages and unemployment was high. People who had stayed in Cuba saw the success that the exiles in America were having and wanted to leave. When a small group of Cubans asked the Peruvian Embassy for asylum in 1980, Castro once again declared that Cubans were free to leave the country if they chose to do so. He opened the port city of Mariel to anyone wanting to *emigrate*. Within days, the crowd at the Peruvian Embassy had grown to 10,000, all wanting to leave Cuba.

The Cuban exiles in Florida made the boat journey to Cuba once more, hoping to bring their relatives home with them. The number of people clamoring to leave Cuba angered Castro. He took prisoners from the jails and the mentally ill from the hospitals and forced them to leave Cuba as well. Over 125,000 Marielitos (MAH-ree-lee-toes), as they were called, made the trip to south Florida without visas. Many observers believe that Castro opened the Mariel port and forced out "undesirables" in response to criticism of Cuba's immigration policy by President Jimmy Carter.

The Marielitos: Twenty-Two Years Later

Among the Marielitos who arrived in America in 1980 were about 650 prisoners and mentally ill patients whom Castro had forced to leave Cuba. Although the United States tried to send them back to Cuba, Castro refused to accept them. These individuals, along with nearly 3,000 Marielitos who were later convicted of crimes, were held in prisons until they could be returned to Cuba. Some of these detainees are still in prisons in the United States twenty-two years later. Although they have served their sentences, they must wait for a review of their case by the INS. Most will eventually be sent back to Cuba.

The U.S. government was faced with a flood of refugees for which it was not prepared. The Cubans who made it to America were, for the most part, poor, unskilled, and black. The news media released story after story describing the new arrivals as hardened criminals. This image followed the Cubans who arrived during this period, making it difficult for the 90 percent who were granted asylum to find work.

A group of Marielitos leave the port of Mariel, Cuba, bound for Florida under the watchful eye of a Cuban army guard.

Today's Cuban Immigrants

Cuban refugees continue to make their way to the United States by any means possible, counting on America's practice of granting asylum to any Cuban who makes it to the United States. New legislation tries to avoid additional mass migrations.

It requires the Coast Guard to stop any Cuban boats bound for the United States at sea and return the passengers to Cuba. In addition, Americans who use their boats to help Cubans enter the country illegally face heavy fines.

Life in America

Cuban Americans are well established in the United States. They are active in government, business, education, and the arts.

Family

The positive experiences of Cuban exiles in America can be traced in large part to the strength of their families, the reasons they came to the United States, and the size of their American communities. Often, several generations—grandparents, parents, and children—would leave Cuba as a group and settle in New York City or Miami, Florida. Fully intending to return to Cuba as soon as Castro was removed from power, these families kept the Cuban culture, including the use of the Spanish language, alive in their homes. These values are reinforced throughout the Cuban community, especially in areas such as Little Havana (so called because Havana is the capital city of Cuba) in Miami. This ability to choose what parts of American culture they want to adapt has been a source of pride for several generations of Cuban Americans.

Fast Facts

•Over 75 percent of all Cuban Americans live in Florida.

•Over half live in the Miami area.

•The Cuban American population in Miami is about the same as the population of Havana, the capital of Cuba.

Work

Cubans are sometimes called "the Golden Exiles" because of the success that they have found in America—far more than any other *immigrant* group. In part, this image is due to the fact that wealthy and middle-class Cubans were the first to arrive in the United States. They formed an *ethnic enclave,* or self-supporting community, in Miami, opening their own businesses and schools. Soon, Little Havana offered many of the same products that the exiles were used to in their native Cuba.

Most of all, the community offered support for the future waves of Cuban exiles and refugees. Even though later arrivals weren't as educated or as financially secure as the first, they were able to make the transition relatively easily (as compared to other refugees, such as the Cambodians). The availability of jobs within the Cuban community helped them adjust to their new surroundings without having to negotiate changes in every area of their life at once.

Another reason for Cuban Americans' position as one of the most upwardly mobile immigrant groups is the acceptance of women in the workforce.

A Cuban American family views plans for its new home. Cuban immigrants have benefited from the economic opportunities available to them in America.

School

The same *ethnic enclaves* that foster entrepreneurship and economic stability for adults provide a secure, insulated school experience for many middle-class Cuban American students. Private Cuban schools are a familiar sight in Miami. Students who attend these schools are protected from any discrimination they might face in public schools. The teachers and principals of these schools, often first-generation immigrants themselves, generally reinforce the values and cultural traditions held by the students' parents. In this situation, role reversal rarely becomes a problem.

Cuban American students in public schools may have more of a struggle to maintain their language and traditions than those in private schools. However, Cuban students report less discrimination overall than any other immigrant group. They are able to adjust to life in America very quickly. Cuban American students have knowledge and expectations of American culture. Many have had relatives living here for years and enjoyed the riches the United States has to offer.

Religion

Before Castro came to power, an estimated 85 percent of Cubans were Roman Catholic. The other 15 percent were Protestant Christians, Jehovah's Witnesses, Jews, and followers of Santería, a blend of West African and Catholic religions. Castro's policies regarding religion have changed through the years. In the early days of his regime, Roman Catholics were often imprisoned or exiled. In the 1980s, Castro allowed people to worship freely again. Pope John Paul II visited Cuba in 1998.

Santería, literally "the way of the saints," developed in Cuba when the Spanish settlers brought in slaves from Africa and baptized them as Roman Catholics. The slaves continued practicing their original religious beliefs, but began associating the different *orishas,* the spirits that rule over nature, with the Catholic saints. In this way, it appeared they were praying to the saints instead of their West African god. Today, Santería is practiced by people of all races and classes, including government leaders and Catholics.

Holidays and Festivals

While some aspects of American life were new to Cubans, holidays seemed very familiar. Most Cubans were Catholic and shared many of the same holidays that are celebrated in the United States. Christmas in Cuba before Castro took control was celebrated in much the same way as in America. Families gathered together to share a traditional feast that often included a roasted pig, black beans, white rice, *yuca con mojo* (yuca in a garlicky citrus sauce), and sweets such as *buñuelos* (fried fritters similar to doughnut holes). Christmas trees, decorated with lights, remained up until gifts were exchanged on January 6, the day that honors the Three King's visit to the baby Jesus. While the celebration on January 6 was more important in Cuba than Christmas Day, Cuban Americans tend to place more emphasis on Christmas Day, when they may have time off from work.

Many Cubans who grew up after Castro came to power didn't share these memories. In 1959, Castro banned American images of Santa Claus at Christmas.

New Year's Day

Families and friends gather again to welcome the New Year with a large family meal. Just before midnight, many Cuban Americans still follow the tradition of eating twelve grapes—one for each month—for good luck.

Calle Ocho Festival

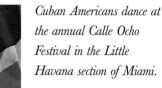

Cuban Americans dance at the annual Calle Ocho Festival in the Little Havana section of Miami.

This unique celebration is one of the largest Hispanic festivals in the United States. Taking its name from the main street of Little Havana where the celebration is held—Eighth Street, or Calle Ocho—the festival began in 1978 as a way of bringing the Hispanic community together. Every March, over a million people gather to enjoy music, dancing, and food from Cuba and other Latin countries.

Calle Ocho (Little Havana)

Many of the early Cuban exiles settled in Miami, Florida. Their community grew around Calle Ocho, or Eighth Street, and became known as Little Havana. Restaurants, markets, and shops featuring Cuban music, food, and cigars made the new immigrants feel at home.

Maximo Gomez Park on Calle Ocho, known to locals as Domino Park, draws many Cuban Americans. They gather to play dominoes, and sometimes chess, in the open air.

Spotlight on
JENNIFER RODRIGUEZ

Cuban American Jennifer Rodriguez races to a bronze medal in the 1,500-meter speed-skating competition at the 2002 Winter Olympics in Salt Lake City, Utah.

Jennifer Rodriguez grew up in South Miami, daughter of a Cuban father and an American mother. She made a name for herself as an inline skater, winning twelve world championships and ten U.S. Festival medals. Then, in 1996, her boyfriend convinced her to switch to speed skating. Two years after stepping onto the ice, Rodriguez qualified for the U.S. speed skating team at the 1998 Winter Olympics in Nagano, Japan, the first American Hispanic athlete to compete in a Winter Olympics.

Rodriguez placed fourth in the 3,000-meter event in the Nagano Olympics, an amazing finish considering her recent entry into the sport. In the 2002 Winter Olympics in Salt Lake City, Rodriguez won the bronze medal in the 1,000- and 1,500-meter events. She holds the American record in the 500-, 1,000-, and 1,500-meter events.

Spotlight On
GUSTAVO PÉREZ FIRMAT

Cuban Americans are well represented in the arts. Many are authors and poets. One of the most famous Cuban American writers is Gustavo Pérez Firmat. Born in Havana, he grew up in Miami, Florida. Although he has written several award-winning books and poetry collections, Pérez Firmat is best known for his book *Next Year in Cuba: A Cubano's Coming of Age in America*. This autobiography was nominated for a Pulitzer Prize in 1995 and was later published in Spanish.

In 1997, *Newsweek* magazine selected Pérez Firmat as one of the "100 Americans to Watch in the Next Century." He was also named as one of the "100 Most Influential" Hispanics in the United States by *Hispanic Business* magazine.

The Arts

Cuban Americans have also made many contributions in the fields of music, cinema, theater, the visual arts, literature, and dance. Many of these artists and performers have entered America's mainstream culture, adding their own distinctive style. Celia Cruz – the "Queen of Salsa" – and Latin jazz musician and bandleader Arturo "Chico" O'Farill are just two of the many Cuban Americans who have contributed to the arts in their adopted country.

Food

Fish, cassava (*yuca*), corn, beans, sweet potatoes, plantains, tomatoes, and pineapples have always been a part of the Cuban diet. Pork and beef are used in many main dishes. These foods, influenced by flavors from the Spanish and African cultures that combined in Cuba, still play an important role in the Cuban diet.

Cuban Americans prepare traditional dishes that feature these foods, along with some specialties that are all their own.

Did You Know?

Desi Arnaz was the first Cuban American to star in a television series. *I Love Lucy*, one of America's most treasured comedy series, almost didn't make it. Producers didn't think American audiences would watch a Cuban American on TV. The success of *I Love Lucy* proved them wrong, paving the way for other Cuban American entertainers such as Andy Garcia.

Cuban sandwiches—made of ham, roasted pork, Swiss cheese, and dill pickles layered inside buttered Cuban bread, pressed, and toasted—are very popular in Cuban American restaurants across the United States. Cuban Americans even have their own Cuban pizza.

Recipe

Plátanos Maduros Fritos (Fried Sweet Plantains)

Vegetable or peanut oil for frying

3 medium-size, very ripe plantains (skin should be black), peeled and sliced diagonally, 1/4-inch thick

In a large skillet, heat 1 inch of oil to 375°F, or until a plantain round sizzles when it touches the oil. Place one layer of plantain rounds in the skillet. Fry until golden brown, 2 to 3 minutes per side, turning with a slotted spoon. Drain on a paper towel–lined platter and serve immediately. (If you are frying a large number of plantains, keep them warm in a 200°F oven until ready to serve.)

Makes 6 servings.

Source: Adapted from Memories of a Cuban Kitchen *by Mary Urrutia Randelman and Joan Schwartz*

CHAPTER SIX

Dominicans

The Dominican Republic,

located southeast of Cuba, occupies two-thirds of the island called Hispaniola. Colonized by Spain in the late fifteenth century, the Dominican path to self-rule has been full of turmoil and upheaval. Once barred from *emigrating* by their government, Dominicans are now one of the largest groups of *immigrants* in the United States.

Americans have received mixed images of Dominicans through the media. Dominicans have been portrayed both as celebrated athletes and as criminals. Immigrants who have worked hard to make a better life for their families in the United States have to work even harder to counteract the negative images.

A Quick Look Back

In 1492, Christopher Columbus landed on the island of Hispaniola. Having set out from Spain to discover a new route to the East Indies (Asia), Columbus thought that he had reached an outlying island off the west coast of India. He called all the islands in the area the "West Indies" and dubbed the native people "Indians." The gold earrings and armbands worn by the native Taino (TIE-no) led Columbus to understand that the island had valuable resources. He claimed the island for Spain.

Spanish Conquest

Spanish settlers arrived within a year. They were given plots of land to farm. The Taino were forced to work in the gold and silver mines Spain had claimed as its own. Within thirty years, the native people had been decimated by disease and overwork.

The Spanish then brought in slaves from Africa to work in the mines. During this period, French settlers established colonies and plantations on the western coast of Hispaniola. In 1697, Spain formally gave the western third of Hispaniola to France; it was later called Haiti. A slave revolt in Haiti in 1791 spread into Santo Domingo, Spain's territory on Hispaniola. Spain surrendered Santo Domingo to France in 1795, but regained control fourteen years later. Haiti victoriously invaded once again, occupying the Spanish *colony* from 1821 to 1843.

Christopher Columbus discovered the island of Hispaniola on his first voyage to the Western Hemisphere. This discovery led to the Spanish conquest of the native Taino people and the introduction of European culture to the island.

Independence

On February 27, 1844, Juan Pablo Duarte led the Spanish colonists of occupied Santo Domingo in a successful revolution against Haiti. The newly independent nation became the Dominican Republic. The early leadership of the Dominican Republic was chaotic. By the late 1800s, the new country had a large foreign debt. The Dominican government feared that other countries would take control of the Dominican Republic if the debt was not paid. The Dominican government asked the United States to help resolve the situation. The resulting agreement called for the United States to help manage the collection of taxes and revenue form imports and exports so the debt could be repaid.

Continuing instability in the Dominican government led the United States to send marines into the Dominican Republic to establish control in 1916. The troops built roads and helped restore order to the economy. The United States gradually turned control of the country back to the Dominicans and withdrew by 1924.

A Dictator Rules

In 1930, General Rafael Leónidas Trujillo (TROO-hee-yo) used intimidation tactics to secure his election.

As a dictator, Trujillo controlled every aspect of Dominican life over the next thirty-one years, even though he did not hold office the entire time. He modernized many aspects of Dominican life, improving roads, expanding ports, building airports, and supporting public education. At the same time, though, Trujillo's secret police kept watch for any criticism of his government or policies. He forced many opponents to leave the country. Others were imprisoned or killed.

Trujillo's practice of not allowing anyone to act against him applied to other countries as well as to Dominicans. In 1937, the Haitian government discovered and executed several of Trujillo's spies. In retaliation, Trujillo ordered that all Haitians residing in the Dominican Republic should be killed. As many as 20,000 Haitians were slaughtered.

After years of controlling a corrupt government, Trujillo was assassinated in mid-1961.

Civil War

At the time of Trujillo's death, Joaquín Balaguer was the Dominican president. The public wanted a new president who had no ties to Trujillo, and Balaguer agreed to step down.

In the first free elections since the 1920s, Juan Bosch Gaviño was elected president. Bosch established a new constitution that limited the power of the Roman Catholic Church and guaranteed new individual rights. Almost immediately, he was accused of being supported by Communists. A group of military officers called a *junta* (HUN-ta) took control of the government in late 1963.

A *civil war* broke out between Bosch supporters (Constitutionalists) and conservative forces on the right (Loyalists). The United States sent troops in to restore order. Elections were held in 1966. Balaguer was returned to office. Under Balaguer's direction, the economy stabilized and even began to grow. He was reelected in 1970 and 1974.

Dressed in his formal army uniform, General Rafael Trujillo delivers a speech.

Recession

When sugar prices fell in the mid-1970s, the Dominican people were hard hit. Unemployment reached new highs. The Dominican Revolutionary Party (Spanish acronym PRD) won the 1978 elections. Although the new president, Silvestre Antonio Guzmán, implemented several economic and social reforms, the nation continued to struggle. Hurricanes in 1979 left hundreds of thousands homeless.

Jorge Blanco, another PRD candidate, was elected president in 1982. He asked for loans from the International Monetary Fund to prop up the Dominican economy. In return for the money, he had to agree to raise prices for food and gasoline. A public outcry greeted this decision. Riots protesting the austerity measures broke out across the country.

With so many people out of work and hungry, many looked to the United States for new opportunities. The United States issued thousands of visas to Dominicans who wished to emigrate. In the view of the U.S. government, it was better to welcome new immigrants than to risk political instability or the rise of Communism in another neighboring country.

Participants in the annual Dominican Festival of Rhode Island make final adjustments to their costumes, known as Diablos Conjulos, *before joining the parade that kicks off this celebration of Dominican culture.*

The Dominican Republic Today

Balaguer returned to power in 1986, serving as president for the next ten years. The PRD regained power in 2000 with the election of Hipólito Mejía. Increased tourism has provided much-needed jobs, but unemployment is still a critical problem.

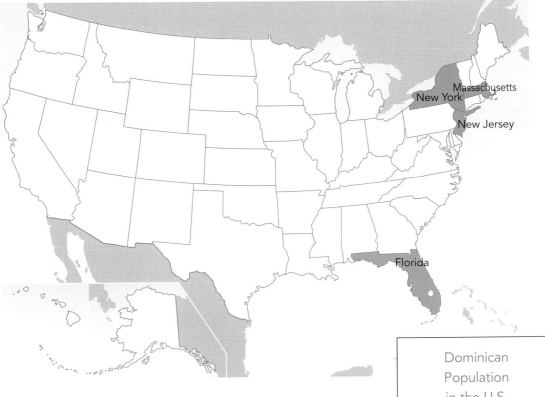

Massachusetts
New York
New Jersey
Florida

Coming to America

Dominican
Population
in the U.S.

New York	369,891
New Jersey	84,512
Massachusetts	56,777
Florida	51,822

Source: U.S. Census, 2000

Before 1960, few American immigrants came from the Dominican Republic. The *dictator* in power there, Rafael Trujillo, would not let anyone leave. Since 1960, the number of Dominicans immigrating to the United States has steadily increased. In the 1960s and 1970s, most immigrants left for political reasons. Immigration to the United States, both legal and illegal, continued to post large numbers throughout the 1980s and 1990s as the Dominican economy weakened. Over half of the families in the Dominican Republic were living in poverty. Middle-class Dominicans, who had enjoyed secure jobs until the 1980s, began emigrating to the United States when they lost their jobs. Today nearly a million Dominicans and Dominican Americans live in the United States and Puerto Rico (an American common-wealth). This number includes an esti-mated 80,000 immigrants who entered the country illegally.

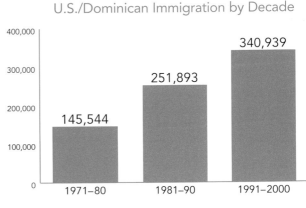

U.S./Dominican Immigration by Decade

Decade	Immigrants
1971–80	145,544
1981–90	251,893
1991–2000	340,939

Source: Statistical Yearbook of the Immigration and Naturalization Service

While both educated and uneducated Dominicans travel to the United States to build a new life for themselves, the majority are unskilled workers. More women emigrate than men, and most are dark-skinned. The latter often have to deal with racial discrimination for the first time when they settle in the United States.

About two-thirds of the Dominican immigrants settle in the New York City area. About one out of eleven New Yorkers are Dominican or Dominican American. The Washington Heights neighborhood in New York City is home to one of the largest Dominican communities in the United States.

Spotlight on SAMMY SOSA

Sammy Sosa gets a hit for the Chicago Cubs. Sosa is one of many successful baseball players who have come to the United States from the Dominican Republic.

The sound of cheering crowds followed Sammy Sosa everywhere in 1998, as he and Mark McGwire battled to break the home run record set by Roger Maris in 1961. First one, then the other would pull ahead in the race. Americans everywhere watched to see who would set the new home run record.

Sammy Sosa was born in a small village near San Pedro de Macoris, Dominican Republic. More professional baseball players come from San Pedro de Macoris than any other town in the world. When baby boys are born in the hospitals there, baseball gloves are placed on their cribs.

Sosa grew up in a poor family. When he was seven years old his father died. Sosa sold orange juice and shined shoes to earn money to help his family. He loved to play baseball, but since he couldn't afford real equipment he improvised. A tree branch became a bat, a rolled-up sock made a ball, and a milk carton was his first glove. Sosa was fourteen years old when he used a real bat for the first time.

Since the Dominican Republic sends more professional baseball players to the United States than any other foreign country, the major league teams send people there every year to watch for new talent. When Sosa was sixteen years old, the Texas Rangers offered him a contract to play ball in the United States.

Sosa's first few years in professional baseball were not his best. He struck out often and averaged only nine home runs per season. The Texas Rangers soon traded him to the Chicago White Sox, who later traded him to the Chicago Cubs. Sosa knew that if he was going to help take care of his family in the Dominican Republic, his game was going to have to improve. He spent a lot of time working on his form. By 1997, Sosa was playing so well that the Cubs offered him a four-year, $42 million contract.

One of baseball's longest lasting records was the home run record set by Roger Maris in 1961 when he hit sixty-one home runs in a single season. In 1998, Sammy Sosa and Mark McGwire of the St. Louis Cardinals battled to break this record. Although McGwire ended up the season with seventy home runs—a new record—Sosa hit sixty-six home runs that year and was named the National League's Most Valuable Player. The next year, Sosa became the first player ever to hit sixty home runs in two different major league seasons.

Sammy Sosa has come a long way from making his own baseball equipment, but he has not forgotten his family or the Dominican Republic. When Hurricane Georges hit the nation in 1998, killing over 200 people, Sosa's foundation raised nearly three-quarters of a million dollars to assist people in his home country.

Life in America

More immigrants come to America from the Dominican Republic than from any other Caribbean nation. Many Dominicans travel between the United States and their homeland frequently. In recent years, Dominican immigrants in the United States have lobbied their government to retain their right to vote in Dominican elections. With this privilege granted, relatively few Dominicans become naturalized American citizens.

Since most Dominican immigrants live in the New York City area, descriptions of how this immigrant group is adapting to life in America will focus on the experiences of this group.

Spotlight on
GUILLERMO LINARES

Mayoral candidate Fernando Ferrer campaigns among the large Dominican community in New York City. City Council member, Guillermo Linares, stands to Ferrer's right.

Guillermo Linares remembers what it was like to grow up on a farm planting crops and taking care of animals. He remembers what it was like to have only one pair of shoes and to carry those shoes as he walked to school, stopping to put them on at the edge of town so they wouldn't get worn out too quickly. He remembers moving from the Dominican Republic to the United States. And he remembers his pride in 1991 when he became the first Dominican American to be elected to public office in the United States.

Linares's mother wanted her children to have a good education, but the village in which they lived had no high school. After considering the options, the family decided to move to the United States so the children could continue their education. His mother *immigrated* to New York City first and was joined later by his father. The family was reunited in 1965, when Linares, along with his brothers and sisters, arrived in the United States. He worked to help his family while attending high school and college.

Linares has a long list of achievements that illustrate his success in his adopted country. Among them: president of Community School Board #6 in New York City; founding member of the Puerto Rican/Latino Education Round Table; founding member and executive director of the Community Association of Progressive Dominicans; and member of the New York City Council. He also served on the President's Advisory Commission on Educational Excellence for Hispanic Americans in 1995.

Guillermo Linares remembers each step he has taken to reach his current position. As he thinks back on his mother and father, who worked so hard to provide opportunities for their nine children, he is filled with pride for his family and his Dominican heritage. He says, "Many people extended their hand to help me along the way. I have never forgotten where I came from. Now it is my job to help other people."

Family

Large, close, extended families are common in the Dominican Republic. They play an important role in the migration of families to the United States as well. Families often send one member at a time to the United States to get established; then that person sends for the next family member and the next. This is called an immigrant chain.

Families are often separated for years while waiting for visas and immigration papers. The extended family that remains on the island takes care of the children until parents are settled. Established immigrants help the newest residents learn English and find a job and a place to live. They help each other with child care. They are also able to gather for meals and share holidays.

Work

In the 1970s, about one-fourth of the immigrants from the Dominican Republic were blue-collar workers before moving to the United States. Only six percent had been employed in professional or technical fields. Less than half of the new immigrants had had an occupation in the Dominican Republic, simply because there were few jobs available there. By the 1980s, the number of people immigrating with work experience had increased, along with the number of Dominicans with professional or technical experience.

Those immigrants who arrived with limited educational backgrounds tended to find jobs in the manufacturing and trade industries. Changes in the manufacturing industry in the 1990s reduced the need for large numbers of workers. This change hit the Dominican American population very hard. About half lost their jobs. Although several smaller companies sprang up to fill the gaps, they often required more education and experience than previous employers and they employed fewer workers.

As a result of these changes in the workplace, more Dominicans began working in service-related jobs, such as restaurants, bars, grocery stores, and clothing and shoe stores. Much of the growth in this job market has been in the suburbs, far from the urban areas where most Dominicans settle.

While unskilled and blue-collar workers often struggle to make a living in the United States, those with professional or technical training and experience have an easier time. Dominican neighborhoods in New York City, such as Washington Heights, have many businesses owned by Dominicans. These entrepreneurs have found an alternative to low-paying jobs by opening businesses such as restaurants, bodegas (grocery stores), clothing and appliance stores, hair salons, insurance agencies, and money transfer services.

A growing number of Dominicans work in professional fields, including business and education. The Dominican-American Chamber of Commerce, the Dominican-American Travel Agents, and the Council of Dominican Educators are just a few of the many organizations that provide support for Dominican professionals in New York City.

Spotlight on
OSCAR DE LA RENTA

Fashion designer Oscar de la Renta shows off a gown from his 2002 collection. The dress is worn by Jacquettea Wheeler, a world-famous model.

Oscar de la Renta, one of the most successful fashion designers ever, was born in the Dominican Republic in 1932. After graduating from high school, he traveled to Europe. While attending art school in Spain, he discovered he had a talent for fashion illustration and pursued a career in that area. Soon he was working for Cristóbal Balenciaga, a famous haute couture designer. (*Haute couture,* "high fashion," refers to very expensive clothing collections that are made for individual customers.)

After working in Paris, de la Renta moved to New York City in 1963 to work for Elizabeth Arden. His main responsibility was the haute couture line, but he convinced Arden that designing ready-to-wear (clothing sold in department stores) would be a good business move. After the initial plans were made, Arden decided not to carry through with the project. The company that was planning to take on Arden's new line hired de la Renta to design his own line of clothing. A year later, in 1966, the label changed to Oscar de la Renta. By 1974, de la Renta and a partner took ownership of the company. Today, that company earns $500 million a year. Oscar de la Renta's designs have been worn by three of America's first ladies: Nancy Reagan, Hillary Clinton, and Laura Bush. His collections of day and evening wear embody a classic, feminine style.

In 1990, de la Renta received the Lifetime Achievement Award from the Council of Fashion Designers of America. But de la Renta was not content with being one of the best-known names in the fashion industry. He has served on the boards of the Metropolitan Opera, Carnegie Hall, and the Americas Society. He established and supports two schools in the Dominican Republic. The schools offer a range of services, including day care centers, classes for blind and deaf children, and health care facilities.

Fast Facts

• Nearly two-thirds of all immigrants from the Dominican Republic live in New York City.

• The Dominican Republic is second only to Mexico in the number of Latin Americans immigrating to the United States.

• The Dominican Republic sends more professional league baseball players to the United States than any other foreign country.

School

School in the United States is often very different from what Dominican children have experienced. Lack of reliable electricity and the poverty of the area generally mean that computers are not available in Dominican schools. In some villages, children may attend school only for four hours in the morning or afternoon, so their first days in an American school seem very long. Learning English is, of course, a top priority for immigrant students who speak only Spanish, but luckily there are often other students in the classroom who can help translate. In addition, many Dominican students are enrolled in English as a Second Language (ESL) or bilingual classes.

One of the problems that many Dominican immigrants have to deal with in America is the quality of the neighborhood schools. With most Dominicans living in large metropolitan areas such as New York City and Miami, children often attend schools that have low math and reading achievement levels, high dropout rates, a large gang presence, and lax discipline. Since many Dominican children arrive in the United States with low levels of schooling, their placement in low-performing schools creates an additional hurdle for them to overcome. As the new arrivals try to fit in with their peers, their school performance may drop or they may begin to use drugs.

A large number of Dominican parents have responded by sending their children back to the Dominican Republic to be educated and disciplined in the traditional manner, although this doesn't happen as frequently as it did in the 1970s and 1980s. According to some estimates, as many as 10,000 students in private schools in the Dominican Republic in the mid-1990s were children of New York City immigrants.

Despite the poor conditions in which Dominican students may find themselves, a number of them overcome the odds, graduating from high school and continuing on to college. Dominican students make up the largest Latino group on several campuses of the City University of New York (CUNY), resulting in the addition of courses related to Dominican heritage.

Religion

Roman Catholicism is the official religion in the Dominican Republic, practiced by nearly all Dominicans. A small percentage of Dominicans are Protestant Christians. About 1 percent practice voodoo, a religion based on ancient African beliefs.

Holidays and Festivals

Christmas is the biggest holiday of the year for most Dominicans. Celebrations take place throughout the month of December. Dominican Americans often return to the island to celebrate Christmas Eve and Christmas Day with family members. The Christmas season ends on January 6, the day that honors the three kings' visit to the baby Jesus. Children traditionally leave a glass of water and a box of hay or grass at the foot of their beds for the kings' camels on the evening of January 5, and the kings leave the children a gift.

In the United States, families often exchange gifts on Christmas Day, but leave their trees up until January 6. Many children eagerly adopt the Santa Claus traditions in America.

The Arts

People around the world have enjoyed Dominican music for years. The most recognizable contribution for most Americans is the merengue (ME-ren-gay). This musical form began as a rural folk dance and later developed into a ballroom dance. While the guitar is the most popular instrument for merengue bands, flutes, marimbas, and percussion instruments such as the tambora drum and guiro are also featured. The merengue was introduced in the United States in the 1920s and gained a large following by the 1950s. By the mid-1980s, merengue had become the most requested music from the Caribbean in the United States.

A new form of music called *bachata* came to life in the Dominican Republic in the 1960s. Featuring the guitar and sad stories about love and life, *bachata* had its roots in Cuban bolero music. Middle- and upper-class Dominicans looked down on the new music. With its crude and often vulgar lyrics, *bachata* was considered to be the music of the poor rural people who lived in shantytowns in the cities.

As Dominican immigrants settled in the United States, these bawdy songs continued to grow in popularity. *Bachata Rose* was recorded in 1991 and released by Juan Luis Guerra and his 4:40 Group. It hit the best seller charts immediately and gained worldwide success. This breakthrough achievement was rewarded in 1992, when *Bachata Rose* won a Grammy award in the Latin Tropical category.

Literature

Dominican American authors have been publishing novels and short stories, poetry, and nonfiction since the early 1900s. Although some writers have reached a mainstream audience, the majority write in Spanish for a mostly Dominican audience.

During the reign of the dictator Trujillo (1930-1961), many writers left the Dominican Republic for the United States, where they could write freely. These authors were, for the most part, from middle-class or well-to-do families who had enjoyed a privileged lifestyle in their home country. Many of today's authors were children who immigrated with their families after the death of Trujillo. This immigrant wave included many poor Dominicans who struggled to build a life for themselves in the United States. Their experiences of adjusting to the American culture are often woven into their work.

Spotlight on
DOMINICAN AMERICAN AUTHORS

Julia Alvarez, an American-born Dominican, has been recognized for her works of poetry and fiction since 1984 when *Homecomings,* a collection of her poetry, was published. Although she gained a widespread audience through her poetic works, Alvarez won national and international awards for her first two novels, *How the García Girls Lost Their Accents* and *In the Time of the Butterflies.*

Junot Díaz came to the United States in the 1970s as a young child. Many of his short stories and novels explore the experiences of Dominicans as immigrants in a less-than-welcoming world. His work has been included in the Houghton Mifflin anthologies *The Best American Short Stories: 1996* and *The Best American Short Stories: 1997.* In addition, Díaz's collection of stories, *Drown,* was recognized as a Notable Book of 1996 by the *New York Times Book Review.*

Dominican-born writer Junot Díaz poses for a portrait in his apartment in Syracuse, New York.

Art

Although Dominican American artists have been creating and exhibiting work in a variety of media for over eighty years, many did not reach a mainstream American audience until recently. In the 1980s, Dominican American artists formed a group that sought out nontraditional locations for exhibitions, such as the Department of Cultural Affairs for the City of New York and corporate headquarters. Soon, the painting, sculpture, and photography of Dominican Americans began to appear in national and international galleries.

A less traditional art form of the urban Dominican communities is memorial art, murals on buildings honoring those who have died in drug-related killings or by some other cause. In most cases, no one knows the names of the people in the painting or the artists.

Food

The food of the Dominican Republic has much in common with that of other Caribbean nations. Cassava (yuca), plantains, taro, sweet potatoes, and yams are basics at many meals, as are beans and rice. Meats such as chicken and goat flavor many Dominican dishes. Longaniza, a pork sausage, is very popular as well. Sancocho, a stew of meat and vegetables, is often called the national dish of the Dominican Republic. Another popular dish, mondongo, combines ham, spices, tripe, and root vegetables into a fragrant soup.

While many of the foods that Dominicans enjoy are available in the United States, they often have a different taste. Juices are processed, rather than fresh-squeezed. Milk is pasteurized and served cold instead of being drunk warm soon after the cow was milked. These small differences serve as one more reminder of how the new immigrants' lives have changed.

Recipe

Sancocho

2 pounds pork loin, cubed

Salt and freshly ground pepper to taste

2 onions, finely chopped

1 leek, chopped

4 cloves garlic, chopped

1 tablespoon each chopped parsley and cilantro

Bay leaf

1 hot pepper, chopped

1 tablespoon vinegar

3 tablespoons Seville (bitter) orange juice, or 1-1/2 tablespoon each orange and lime juice

1 pound longaniza sausage or Italian sweet sausage, fried and sliced

2 green plantains, peeled and sliced in 2-inch pieces

1 pound each yuca (cassava), yautia (taro root), calabaza (West Indian pumpkin), sweet potatoes, and yams, peeled and diced into 1-inch cubes

3 ears corn, each cut into 3 pieces

Put the pork in a heavy 4-quart soup pot. Season with salt and pepper. Add the onions, leek, garlic, parsley, cilantro, bay leaf, hot pepper, vinegar, and bitter orange juice and enough water to barely cover the meat. Bring to a boil, then reduce heat, cover, and simmer over low heat for about an hour.

Add the sausage, plantains, and vegetables to the soup pot. Bring to a boil, then cover and simmer 45 minutes or until all the ingredients are tender.

Serves 6–8.

Source: Adapted from Recipe Archives
©2001 Stephanie da Silva
http://recipes.alastra.com/caribbean/sancocho01.html
and A Taste of Puerto Rico *by Yvonne Ortiz*

Glossary

amnesty a government pardon for a crime

assimilation the process of changing one's traditions to fit into a new culture

asylee a person who asks for asylum upon entry to the United States. Asylees may have entered the United States legally or illegally, but they have to meet the same requirements as refugees before they are granted asylum

asylum protection or safety from persecution or the threat of persecution

cartel a group of drug sellers who join together to control the drug trade

civil war a war fought within one country

colony an area or country under the control of another country

Communism a system of government in which the state plans and controls the economy and a single, often authoritarian party holds power, claiming to make progress toward a higher social order in which all goods are equally shared by the people

Communist a person who supports Communism

coup a takeover of the government, usually by military leaders

decentralized describing a government in which the power is shared, usually between the federal and state levels

deport to send a person back to his or her home country

dictator a leader who rules a country through force, often imprisoning or killing those who speak out against the government

emigrate to leave one country to live in another

emigration the process of moving to another country

ethnic enclave an area within a city that is settled by people who share a common ethnic heritage, such as Little Havana in Miami, Florida

exile a person who has to live in another country, usually for political reasons

famine a severe shortage of food

fundamentalist describing a strict religious movement based on a literal reading of holy texts

genocide a deliberate attempt to kill everyone in a particular racial, political, or cultural group

guerrillas people who work in small groups to attack their enemies, usually the government

immigrant a person who moves from one country to live in another

immigrate to come to a country with plans to live there

land mine a buried device that explodes when touched or stepped upon

mujahideen Islamic guerrilla fighters

nativism a feeling that the economic and political interests of a country's citizens are more important than those of its legal immigrants

naturalization the process a legal immigrant goes through to become an American citizen

quota system a system of determining how many immigrants can enter a country each year. In this system, a foreign country or region is assigned a quota, or maximum number of immigrants.

rebellion armed resistance against authority, usually unsuccessful

refugee a person who seeks safety in another country due to fears of imprisonment, torture, or death because of race, religion, nationality, or political beliefs. In the United States, refugee status is granted to those who apply for resettlement in the United States while they are still in another country

regime a particular style of government; often used to describe a government that controls its people through force or oppression

resettled to be moved to a new home in a different country

terrorists individuals or groups who use violence to intimidate or influence others, especially for political reasons

Bibliography

AfghanCrisis.com
www.afghancrisis.com

Afghanistan Online
www.afghan-web.com

Afghan Network
www.afghan-network.net

Afghanpedia www.sabawoon.com/afghanpedia/default.shtm

Afropop Worldwide: Celebrating the Musical Cultures of Africa and the African Diaspora, "Cumbia"
http://www.afropop.org/explore/show_style/ID/31/cumbia/

Ali, Sharifah Enayat. *Afghanistan*. New York: Marshall Cavendish, 1995.

Ashabranner, Brent K. *Our Beckoning Borders: Illegal Immigration to America*. New York: Cobblehill/Dutton, 1996.

——. *Still a Nation of Immigrants*. New York: Cobblehill/Dutton, 1993.

Blonder, Ellen, and Annabel Low. *Every Grain of Rice: A Taste of Our Chinese Childhood in America*. New York: Clarkson Potter, 1998.

Bode, Janet. *The Colors of Freedom: Immigrant Stories*. New York: Franklin Watts, 2000

——. *New Kids in Town: Oral Histories of Immigrant Teens*. New York: Scholastic, 1995.

Brownstone, David M., and Irene M. Franck. *Facts about American Immigration*. New York: H.W. Wilson, 2001.

Café de Colombia
www.juanvaldez.com

Cambodia: Beauty and Darkness; The Odyssey of the Khmer People
www.mekong.net/Cambodia

"Cambodian Celebrates New Year with Buddha," *Merit Times*, 4/17/02. www.english.hsilai.org/merittimes/detail.asp?index=6171&page=B

Cameron, Sara. *Out of War: True Stories from the Front Lines of the Children's Movement for Peace in Colombia*. New York: Scholastic, 2001.

Canesso, Claudia. *Cambodia*. Philadelphia: Chelsea House, 1999.

Carvin, Andy. From Sideshow to Genocide: Stories of the Cambodian Holocaust
http://edwebproject.org/sideshow/

Central Pacific Railroad Photographic History Museum, "Chinese-American Contribution to Transcontinental Railroad."
http://cprr.org/Museum/Chinese.html

Chinese American Museum in Los Angeles
http://www.camla.org/

Chinese Culture Center of San Francisco
www.c-c-c.org

Chinese Historical and Cultural Project
http://www.chcp.org/

Chinese Music
http://www.regenttour.com/china/music/index.htm

CNN. Soldiers of God, 1975-1988
www.cnn.com/SPECIALS/cold.war/episodes/20/

Currie, Stephen. *Issues in Immigration*. San Diego: Lucent Books, 2000.

Daley, William. *The Chinese Americans*. New York: Chelsea House, 1996.

Davis, Patty. "Cuban-Americans Struggle with Memories of Childhood Airlifts." *CNN Interactive,* 1/12/98
www.cnn.com/US/9801/12/pedro.pan/

Dawson, Mildred Leinweber. *Over Here It's Different: Carolina's Story*. New York: Macmillan, 1993.

De Monteiro, Longteine, and Katherine Neustadt. *The Elephant Walk Cookbook*. New York: Houghton Mifflin, 1998.

Embassy of Colombia http://www.colombiaemb.org

Federico-O'Murchu, Sean. "22 Years Later, Cubans in Legal Limbo." *MSNBC News,* 5/10/02
http://www.msnbc.com/news/ 749423.asp

Flesher, Paul. Exploring Religions, University of Wyoming Religious Studies Program
http://uwacadweb.uwyo.edu/religionet/er/default.htm

Foley, Erin. *Dominican Republic*. New York: Marshall Cavendish, 1997.

Forero, Juan. "Prosperous Colombians Fleeing, Many to the U.S." *New York Times,* 4/10/01 istsocrates.berkeley.edu/~border/list_articles/041001_nytimes_colombia.html

formula1.com. "Driver Bio: Juan Montoya." www.formula1.com/drivers/h826.html

Gay, Kathlyn. *Leaving Cuba: From Operation Pedro Pan to Elian.* Brookfield, CT: Twenty-First Century Books, 2000.

Genz, Michelle. "Golden Girl." *Miami Herald,* 5/31/98 http://www.fiu.edu/~fcf/gloria 53198.html

Gow, Catherine Hester. *The Cuban Missile Crisis.* San Diego: Lucent Books, 1997.

Graff, Nancy Price. *Where the River Runs: A Portrait of a Refugee Family.* Boston: Little, Brown, 1993.

Herda, D.J. *The Afghan Rebels: The War in Afghanistan.* New York: Franklin Watts, 1990.

HGSE News (Harvard Graduate School of Education). "85% of Immigrant Children Experience Separation During Migration Process." 6/29/01 http://www.gse.harvard.edu/news/features/suarez06292001.html

Hoobler, Dorothy, and Thomas Hoobler. *The Chinese American Family Album.* New York: Oxford University Press, 1994.

——. *The Cuban Family Album.* New York: Oxford University Press, 1996.

Karoff, Barbara. *South American Cooking: Foods and Feasts from the New World.* Berkeley, CA: Aris Books, 1989.

Keo, Sopheap. "Child-Rearing and Discipline among Cambodian Americans." Khmer Institute http://www.khmerinstitute.org/

Kim, Hyung-chan, ed. *Distinguished Asian Americans.* Westport, CT: Greenwood Press, 1999.

Kite, Lorien. *The Chinese.* New York: Crabtree, 2000.

Lee, Kathleen. *Illegal Immigration.* San Diego: Lucent Books, 1996.

Luke Powell—Photographs cr.middlebury.edu/art/Powell/

Maniatis, Gregory A. "Tribal Counsel." New York Magazine, October 22, 2001.

McDermott, Jeremy. "Colombia's Rebel Kidnappers." BBC News, 1/7/02 http://news.bbc.co.uk/1/hi/world/americas/1746914.stm

Méndez, Adriana. *Cubans in America.* Minneapolis: Lerner Publications, 1994.

Michels, Spencer. "Afghan Americans Look Homeward." *Online NewsHour PBS,* 1/7/02. http://www.pbs.org/newshour/bb/asia/jan-june02/homeward_1-07.html

Microsoft Encarta Online Encyclopedia 2002. "Afghanistan" http://encarta.msn.com

——. "Cambodia"

——. "Confucianism"

——. "Confucius"

——. "China"

——. "Cuba"

——. "Dominican Republic"

Morrison, Marion. *Colombia.* New York: Children's Press, 1999.

Moscoso, Claudia. "Colombians Flee War-Torn Land, Find New Home in Florida." *Dayton-Beach News-Journal,* 9/5/02 www.news-journalonline.com/2002/Sep/5/WVOL1.htm

Museum of the City of San Francisco http://www.sfmuseum.org/

Myers, Aaron. "Santería" www.africana.com

National Association of Hispanic Journalists http://www.nahj.org/resourceguide/intro1.html

National Immigration Forum. "Cycles of Nativism in U.S. History." http://www.immigrationforum.org/pubs/articles/cyclesofnativism2001.htm

Phal, Chakriya, and Hun Ly. "Survey on Cambodian American Family and Gender Issues." *Khmer Institute* www.khmerinstitute.org/

Portes, Alejandro, and Rubén G. Rumbaut. *Legacies.* Berkeley: University of California Press, 2001.

Randelman, Mary Urrutia, and Joan Schwartz. *Memories of a Cuban Kitchen.* New York: Macmillan, 1992.

Rumbaut, Rubén G., and Alejandro Portes. *Ethnicities.* Berkeley: University of California Press, 2001.

Shakira
http://www.shakira.com

Sharp, Bruce. "Chan Khoun: Cover Story," 1990. *An edited version originally appeared in the Providence Journal-Bulletin.* www.mekong.net/cambodia/chan.htm

She, Colleen. *Teenage Refugees from China Speak Out.* New York: Rosen Publishing Group, 1995.

Shipley, Amy. "Out of Miami, Rodriguez Is Warming to Ice." *Washington Post,* 2/2/98.

Skerry, Peter. "Do We Really Want Immigrants to Assimilate?" *Society,* March, 2000 (found online at The Brookings Institution) http://www.brook.edu/views/articles/skerry/2000societymarapr.htm)

Takaki, Ronald. *From Exiles to Immigrants: The Refugees from Southeast Asia.* New York: Chelsea House, 1995.

Thornburgh, Nathan. "Behind the Lens: Art and Identity for Cambodian-American Girls in Seattle." *Phnom Penh Post,* Issue 10/23, November 9–22, 2001. http://www.speakeasy.org/~nthorn/phnompenh.html

Ung, Loung. "Children of the Holocaust, Children of the Killing Fields," transcript of a speech made 7/20/00 at the Spertus Museum of Judaica, Chicago (text found at www.mekong.net/cambodia/children.html)

United Nations High Commissioner for Refugees (UNHCR). "Afghan Refugee Statistics 10 Sep 2001" http://www.reliefweb.int/w/rwb.nsf/vID/81F3C45318379FABC1256ACB0039B878?OpenDocument

U.S. Immigration and Naturalization Service. *Statistical Yearbook of the Immigration and Naturalization Service,* 1978, 1980, 1982, 1984, 1986, 1988, 1994,1996, 2000. Washington, D.C: Government Printing Office. www.ins.gov

U.S. Speedskating http://www.usspeedskating.org/rosters/Rodriguez.html

Wang, Wei-Min. "Resistance to the Anti-Chinese Movement, 1952-1905: The Chinese American Perspective" http://uts.cc.utexas.edu/~lpaj144/tk/thesis/contents.html

Williams, Mike. "While Summit Dwells on Trade, Colombians Live in Fear." *Cox News,* 4/20/01 www.coxnews.com/washingtonbureau/staff/williams/04-20-01 COLOMBIA AMERICAS0420COX1ST.html

Young, Grace. *The Wisdom of the Chinese Kitchen: Classic Family Recipes for Celebration and Healing.* New York: Simon & Schuster, 1999.

Index